West Coast Main Line Locomotive Haulage

ANDY FLOWERS

BRITAIN'S RAILWAYS SERIES, VOLUME 24

Contents page image: 86612 and 86312 at Cathiron on a Freightliner service to Daventry International Freight Terminal on 2 May 2020. The locos only had a few more months in service at this stage.

Published by Key Books
An imprint of Key Publishing Ltd
PO Box 100
Stamford
Lincs PE19 1XQ

www.keypublishing.com

The right of Andy Flowers to be identified as the author of this book has been asserted in accordance with the Copyright, Designs and Patents Act 1988 Sections 77 and 78.

Copyright © Andy Flowers, 2021

ISBN 978 1 80282 030 0

All rights reserved. Reproduction in whole or in part in any form whatsoever or by any means is strictly prohibited without the prior permission of the Publisher.

Typeset by SJmagic DESIGN SERVICES, India.

Contents

Introduction 4

Chapter 1 Infrastructure 7

Chapter 2 Service Development 15

Chapter 3 Steam Traction 25

Chapter 4 Diesel Prototypes 44

Chapter 5 The Diesel Era – Type 1s 47

Chapter 6 Electric Locomotives 67

Chapter 7 Records & Performance 92

Chapter 8 New Operators 95

Introduction

With a long and interesting history, this book can only give a flavour of the West Coast Main Line (WCML) and the varied range of traction that has graced it. The first sections were completed as part of a triangle serving the industrial cities of the northwest and the Midlands, namely Liverpool, Manchester, and Birmingham. The Grand Junction Railway linked Birmingham with the Liverpool and Manchester Railway at Newton, making the section between Stafford and Warrington the first portion of the West Coast Main Line to be built. The line heralded the opening of the London and Birmingham Railway, completing a through connection between London and the northern cities.

The core London–Glasgow route comprises 399 miles and, with a number of major branches, total track mileage adds up to around 700 miles. Like most main routes, the WCML was built by several pre-grouping companies, which were amalgamated in 1923 as part of the LMS then nationalised in 1948 under BR. Privatisation followed in the 1990s, then renationalisation under Network Rail in the 2000s, and today in public ownership with private franchises operating local, regional and inter-city services.

The first section of the route, from Warrington to Birmingham, opened on 6 July 1837 purely as a connection southward from the Liverpool and Manchester Railway at Newton. On 20 July, the first section was opened out of Euston as far as Boxmoor, later to be renamed Hemel Hempstead. The whole London and Birmingham Railway through to Curzon Street was opened by 20 September 1838, completing a through route from London to Preston via Birmingham. Curzon Street closed for passengers in 1854 when New Street was opened. Rationalisation of ownership of the route took place in July 1846 with the London and North Western Railway (LNWR), formed from the amalgamation of the Grand Junction Railway (which had already absorbed the Liverpool and Manchester) together with the London and Birmingham and Manchester and Birmingham railways.

Development of the WCML north of Preston was challenging, with the hills of Cumbria and the Scottish Borders in the way. The Lancaster and Carlisle Railway performed miracles to construct its route by 1846, only two years after incorporation. There was debate over the best route with alternatives considered by George Stephenson and Joseph Locke. Locke proposed tunnelling under

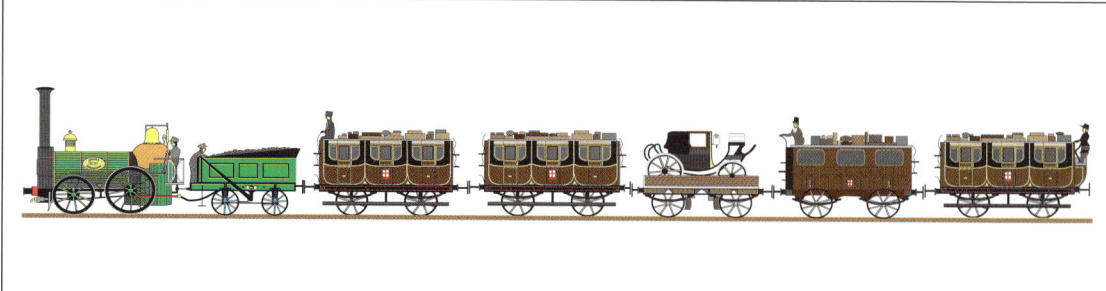

A typical consist for an early Victorian mixed passenger service between London Euston and Birmingham Curzon Street from around 1840. The open wagon carrying a Regency era Travel Chariot is perhaps an early precursor of the 20th century Motorail services. The loco, No 28, is a Bury 2-2-0.

Introduction

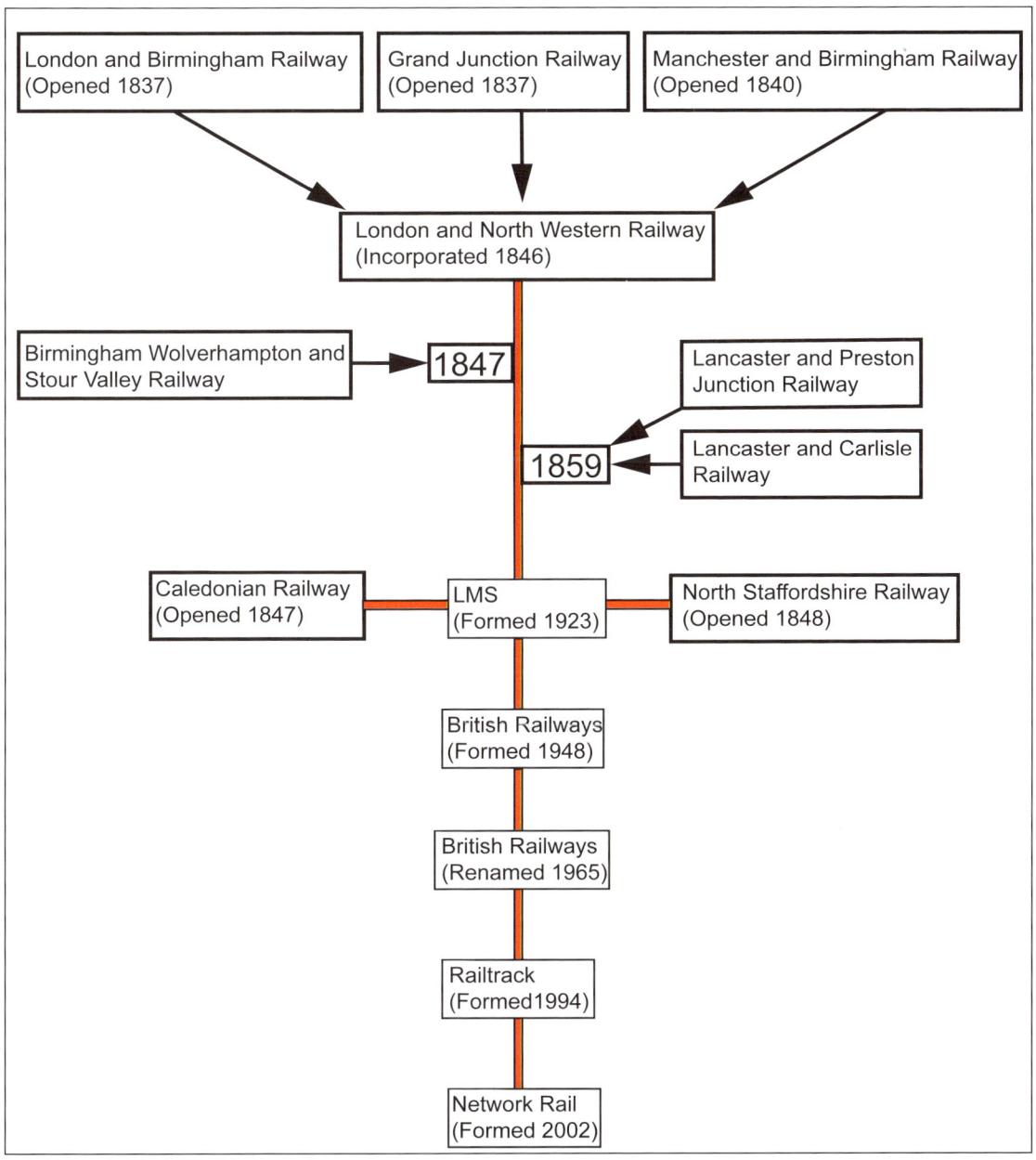

Shap with two alternative routes between Tebay and Penrith while Stephenson favoured avoiding the hills, going around the Cumbrian Coast with a barrage across Morecambe Bay between Humphrey and Poulton. Traffic potential from Kendal was a major factor and the railway was built through the Fells, in accordance with Locke's plan. The direct (Trent Valley) route to the north opened in 1847, avoiding the West Midlands industrial conurbations.

After completion of the Lancaster and Carlisle Railway, opening of a through London to Glasgow route followed weeks later in February 1848 when the Caledonian Railway opened its Annandale Line, from the border ten miles south to Carlisle. Before the opening, the fastest way from London to Glasgow was by LNWR to Liverpool for boat onwards. In 1859, the LNWR gained control from Euston to Carlisle, signing a 999-year lease for the Lancaster and Carlisle, and in 1879, it was formally amalgamated into the LNWR.

The LNWR opened Weaver Junction to Ditton Junction in 1869, completing the WCML as we now know it in 1881 with the Northampton loop. Other major openings included the Trent Valley Railway (direct from Rugby to Stafford via Nuneaton) and the Manchester and Birmingham Railway (from Manchester to Crewe). All these minor companies merged in 1846 under the London and North Western Railway. Smaller companies, including the North Union Railway (from Wigan to Preston), the Lancaster and Preston Junction Railway and the Lancaster and Carlisle Railway were absorbed into the LNWR; in 1889 for the NUR and 1879 for the LPJR and L&C, respectively. In Scotland, the Caledonian Railway opened Carlisle to Beattock in 1847, following on to Edinburgh on 1 April 1848 and Glasgow in 1849.

The Caledonian Railway formed an alliance with the LNWR, enabling through running between Glasgow and London. Like collaborative running between London and Edinburgh over the East Coast Main Line (ECML), trains from London to Glasgow used 'Joint Stock', shared between the LNWR and the Caledonian Railway. The first through trains in the 1850s took over 12.5 hours from London to Glasgow. In 1864, the LNWR opened a direct line from Golborne Junction to Winwick Junction, avoiding the short stretch of the Liverpool and Manchester Railway. South of the border, one small railway company resisted the LNWR, this being the North Staffordshire Railway, connecting Macclesfield to Stafford and Colwich, and which was fiercely independent until the grouping.

Photographed at an unknown location in late Victorian times, 2-4-0T LNWR 'Chopper Tank' 161 is seen in its original configuration without a fully enclosed cab (often described as half-cabbed). Fifty of the Webb-designed type were produced at Crewe between 1876 and 1880. The locos were used mainly on local passenger work around Manchester and Birmingham. After rebuilding, including the addition of full cabs, 16 of the class passed into LMS ownership after the grouping. (Andy Flowers Collection)

Chapter 1
Infrastructure

In 1837, Euston was a two-platform station, complete with impressive classic Doric Arch entrance. Entrance and departure from Euston were designed to avoid bottlenecks, with a track layout of departure lines and burrowing junctions. Traffic flows well at Euston, often freer than at its rival King's Cross. Before powerful locos were available, trains leaving Euston were hauled by rope up the

West Coast Main Line Locomotive Haulage

steep Camden incline to Chalk Farm. The line climbs gradually north as far as Tring before gentle gradients follow.

North of Watford, the route follows the Grand Union Canal to Rugby, while Northampton was originally only served by a branch from Blisworth. The West Coast was built avoiding tunnels and viaducts where possible. Kilsby Tunnel, near Rugby, is the longest on the WCML at 1.25 miles and also the most problematic with a geological fault creating water issues. The section between Crewe and Stafford was built with steeper grades, as the builders were anticipating the introduction of more powerful locomotives. The line climbs at up to 1 in 177 up to the summit at Whitmore. In Scotland, later loco developments enabled the climb of 1 in 70 up Beattock Bank, thereby negating the need for a lengthy avoiding route with viaducts and tunnels.

The WCML brought the development of Crewe by the Grand Junction Railway, this growing from the small village of Church Coppenhall into a major town named after Crewe Hall, with the largest locomotive works in the world. It became a significant junction station with two major motive power sheds, Crewe North for passenger locos and Crewe South, which was mostly for freight.

Route Description

Euston station, now a sprawling 18-platform development with commercial premises, has changed from its earliest days. A few initial platforms were added before redevelopment in the 1960s, including removal of the Doric Arch entrance. A steep gradient starts from the end of the platforms and, until 1844, trains were cable hauled up Camden Bank, although this goes unnoticed by today's traction. Even sleeper services, loaded to 16 vehicles, pose little problems for the Class 92s.

At the top of Camden Bank, the main depot for Euston, Camden shed, was closed to steam in September 1963 and outright in January 1966 upon completion of electrification. London Overground Euston to Watford lines (previously known as the DC lines) are on the right from

In 2002, an HST set led by power car 43180 is seen near Dillicar, just south of Tebay. The grand scale and the beautiful colours of the Northern Fells along this section of the West Coast line are seen to great effect. The imposing nature and disruption of the road traffic caused by the M6 in the background contrasts with the relatively unobtrusive railway. Virgin CrossCountry had 57 power cars for its extensive network, and this service from Penzance to Edinburgh was a typical working for the fleet. By 2008, CrossCountry services would no longer serve Carlisle and trains for Glasgow and Edinburgh are now all routed via the East Coast Main Line. (Andy Flowers Collection)

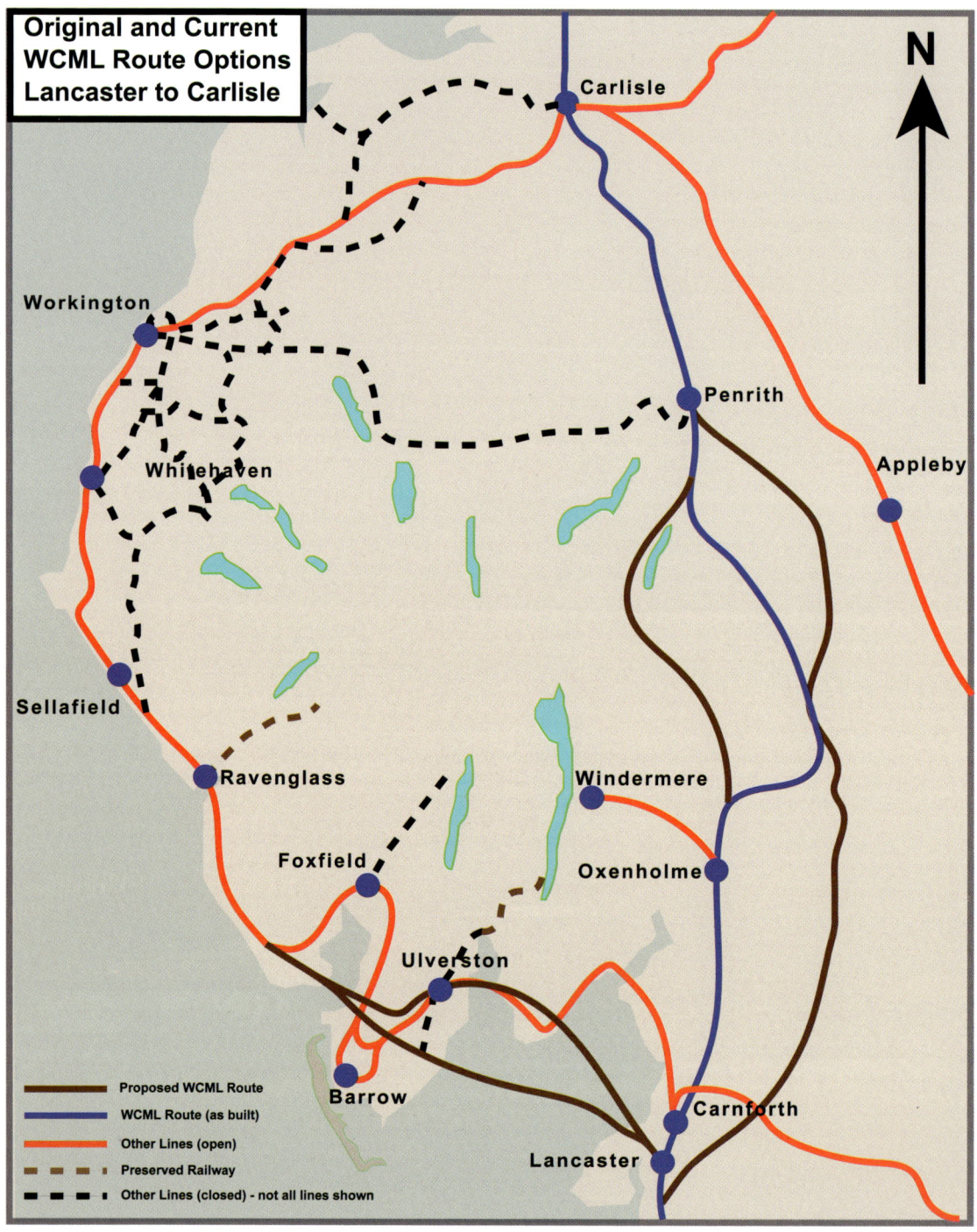

South Hampstead, passing behind Willesden depot and Wembley Yard before crossing under the WCML to the left-hand side, just north of Wembley Yard. After the Royal Mail's Princess Royal Distribution Centre, the line goes past Wembley Yard, a major freight hub and southern base for the Caledonian Sleeper.

Infrastructure

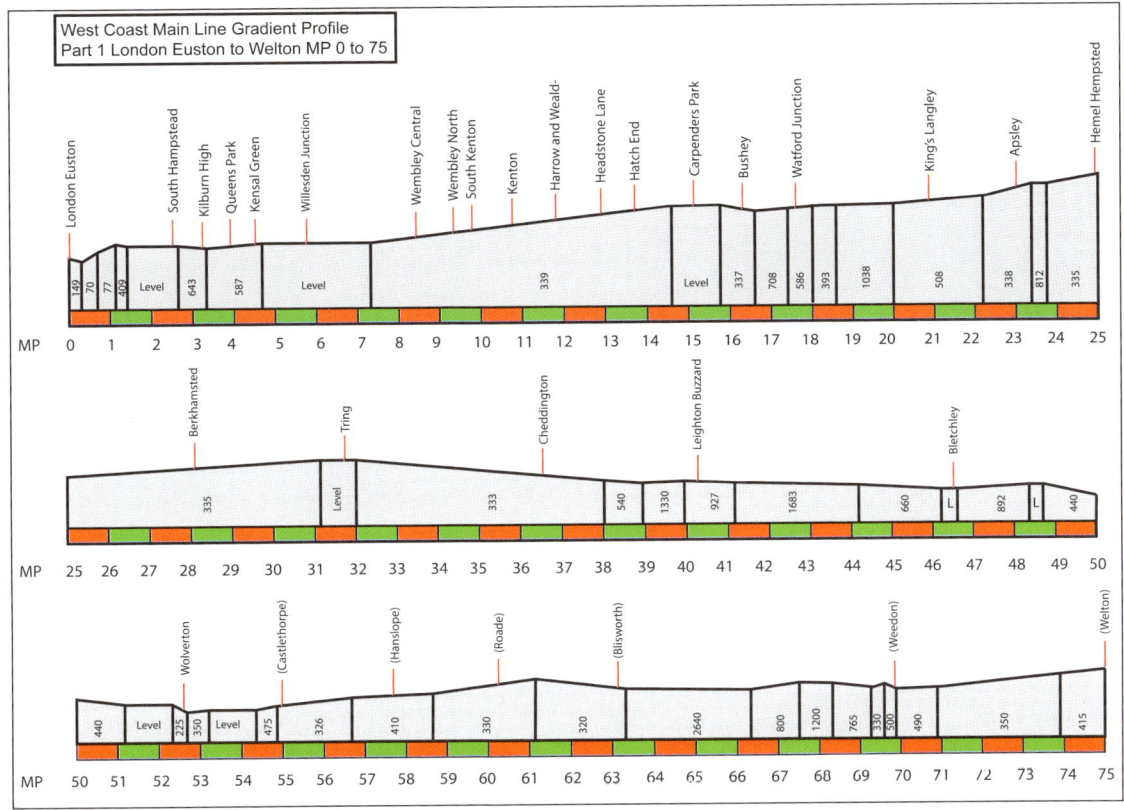

Past Watford, the line climbs gradually into the Chilterns to Tring, within the valley of the River Gade. Tring Cutting, the chalk summit of the Chiltern Ridge, was the biggest civil engineering project on the route. It was built to accommodate two lines and widened to three in 1859 and finally four lines in 1876. The reduced Wolverton Works can be seen on the left after Milton Keynes, where some work is still carried out. The main line originally went through the middle of the works. The line crosses the Ouse over Wolverton Viaduct before a climb to the Northamptonshire uplands and summit at Roade, where the slow lines head right for Northampton.

The M1 is on the left between Weedon and Welton with the Grand Union Canal and all three are side by side near Watford Gap services. Upon diverging from the motorway, the line passes through the 1.4-mile (2.2km) Kilsby Tunnel, one of the major engineering works on the line, with the watershed of rivers running from this ridge west to the Bristol Channel and east to the North Sea. On opening in 1838, this was the longest railway tunnel in the world, originally being single track but expanded to double track in 1879. At Rugby, a flying junction sees the Stour Valley line via Birmingham join on the right.

At Colwich Junction, the line for Manchester via Stoke diverges to the right. Shortly after passing through Shugborough Tunnel, line speed is reduced to 75mph (85mph tilt-enabled) for Queensville Curve approaching Stafford, where the Grand Junction main line from Birmingham joins on the left. Shugborough Tunnel is the last tunnel on the northbound West Coast Main Line until a short section at Eglinton Street approaching Glasgow Central. At a distance of around 270 miles, this was a great feat of engineering on a route over the Cumbrian Fells and the mountains of the Southern Uplands.

From Stafford, the line climbs to a summit at Whitmore before dropping down into Crewe, a complex junction station, although a decrease in freight in recent years has eased the flow of passenger traffic. The Independent Lines that bypass, and in part pass under, the main station

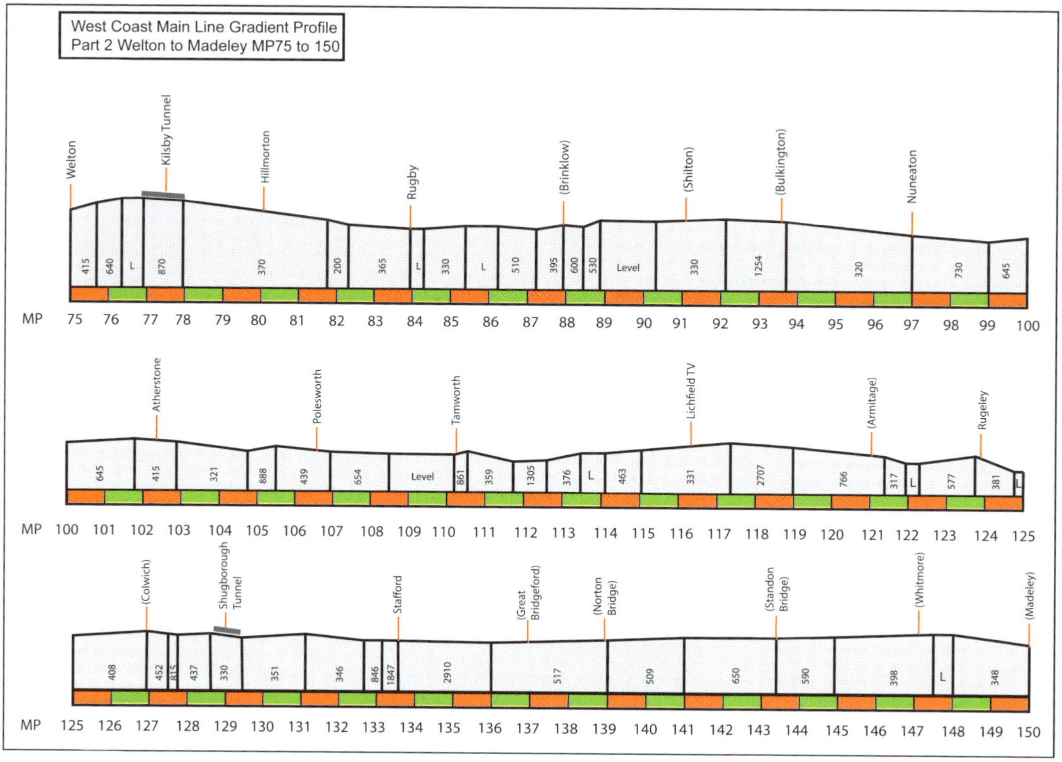
West Coast Main Line Gradient Profile
Part 2 Welton to Madeley MP75 to 150
Welton
Kilsby Tunnel
Hillmorton
Rugby
(Brinklow)
(Shilton)
(Bulkington)
Nuneaton
Atherstone
Polesworth
Tamworth
Lichfield TV
(Armitage)
Rugeley
(Colwich)
Shugborough Tunnel
Stafford
(Great Bridgeford)
(Norton Bridge)
(Standon Bridge)
(Whitmore)
(Madeley)
MP

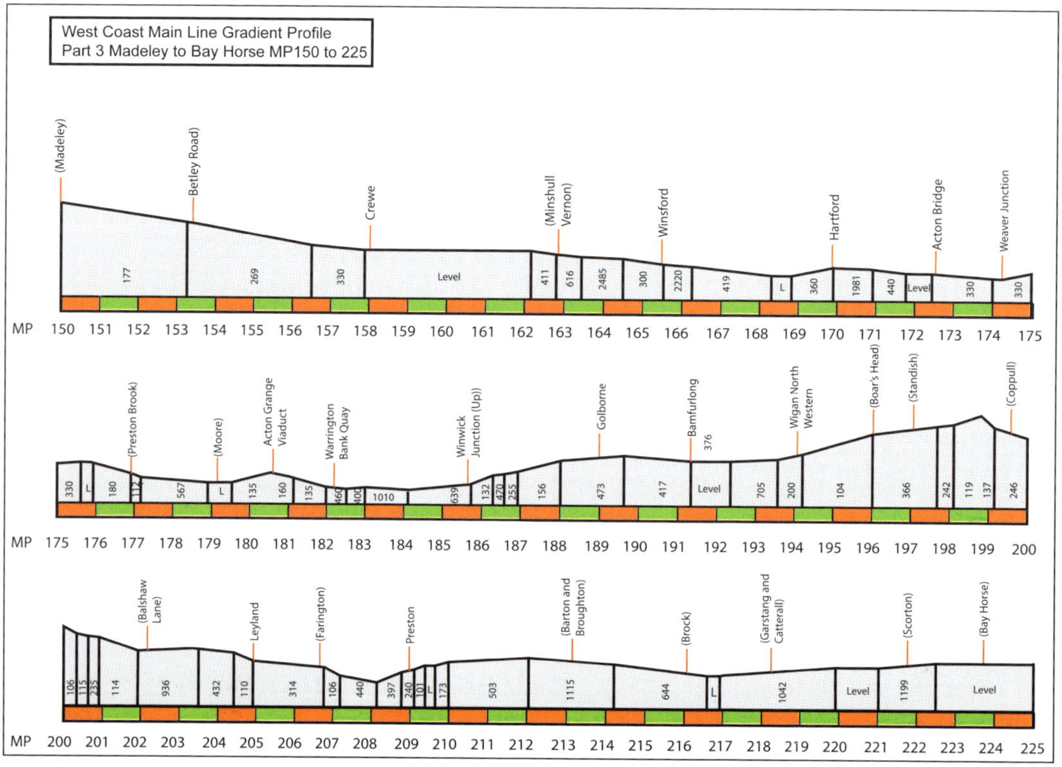
West Coast Main Line Gradient Profile
Part 3 Madeley to Bay Horse MP150 to 225
(Madeley)
Betley Road)
Crewe
(Minshull Vernon)
Winsford
Hartford
Acton Bridge
Weaver Junction
(Preston Brook)
(Moore)
Acton Grange Viaduct
Warrington Bank Quay
Winwick Junction (Up))
Golborne
Bamfurlong
Wigan North Western
(Boar's Head)
(Standish)
(Coppull)
(Balshaw Lane)
Leyland
(Farington)
Preston
(Barton and Broughton)
(Brock)
(Garstang and Catterall)
(Scorton)
(Bay Horse)
MP

also ease the throughput of traffic. Northwards, the line traverses the Cheshire Plain, crossing the River Weaver on Dutton Viaduct with the branch to Liverpool diverging westwards at Weaver Junction. This is a famous example of a flying junction with up trains crossing the main line before joining on the east side. From here, the line climbs at up to 1 in 135 to cross the Manchester Ship Canal.

Three miles after Warrington, the line passes Winwick Junction where lines to Newton-le-Willows (passing the former site of the English Electric plant) and Earlestown diverge to the left, passing under the original Liverpool and Manchester main line where the Grand Junction route south to Birmingham opened in 1837. From Golborne Junction, the line follows the course of the former Wigan branch of the Liverpool and Manchester Railway. Entering Preston, the complex track layout requires a limit of 15mph, while north of Preston the line runs close to sea level with shallow gradients. At Lancaster, the castle can be seen on a hill to the right overlooking the station as the WCML passes along the shoreline mudflats of Morecambe Bay, past Hest Bank.

The Scottish border is crossed at Gretna, eight miles north of Carlisle, and from here the line climbs steadily again, including the most challenging stretch of the whole route. This is ten miles at 1 in 77 from after the site of Beattock station up to the 1,016ft summit at Beattock. From this point, the line drops down into the Clyde Valley and the former industrial areas south-east of Glasgow.

Carstairs State Hospital can be seen to the east of the station. This fortified site is equivalent to the English Broadmoor. Drivers' legend stated that trains would not stop at Carstairs of an evening if a single passenger carrying a suitcase was waiting. A triangular junction was built at Carstairs to enable attachment and detachment of portions and through services between Glasgow and Edinburgh. The line for Aberdeen and Inverness diverges off to the right at Law Junction, just south of Motherwell. The

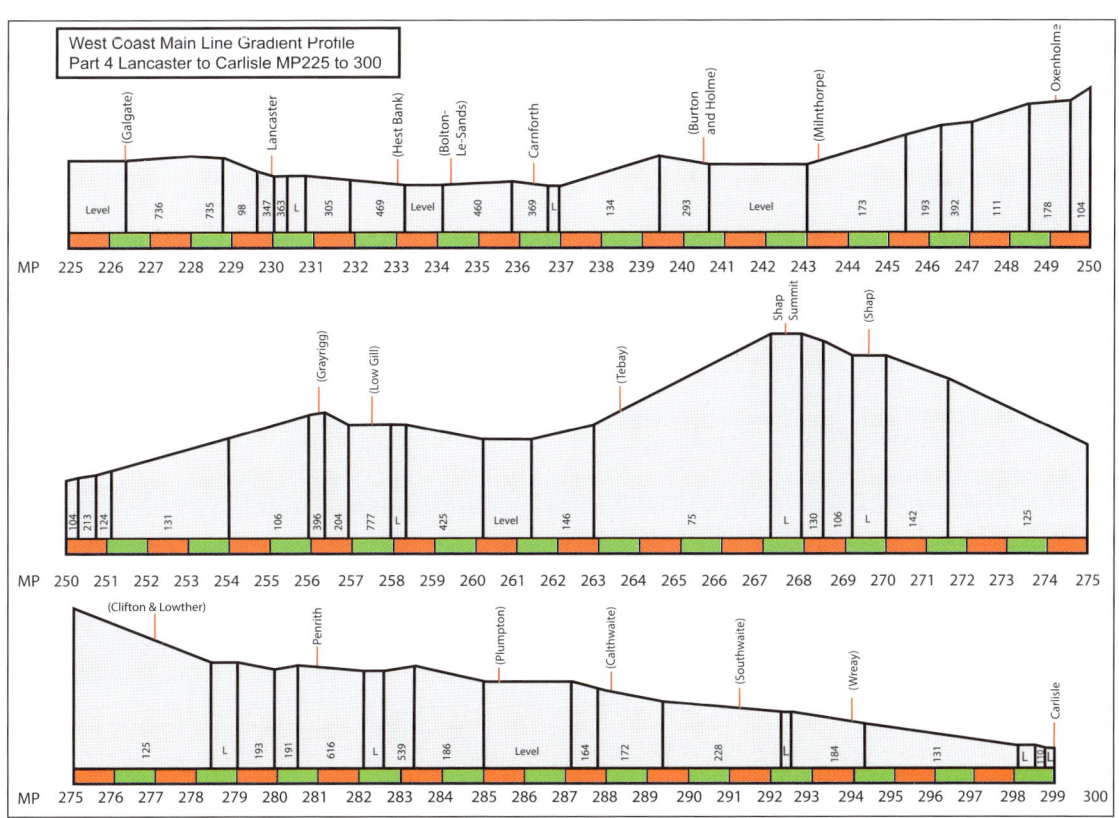

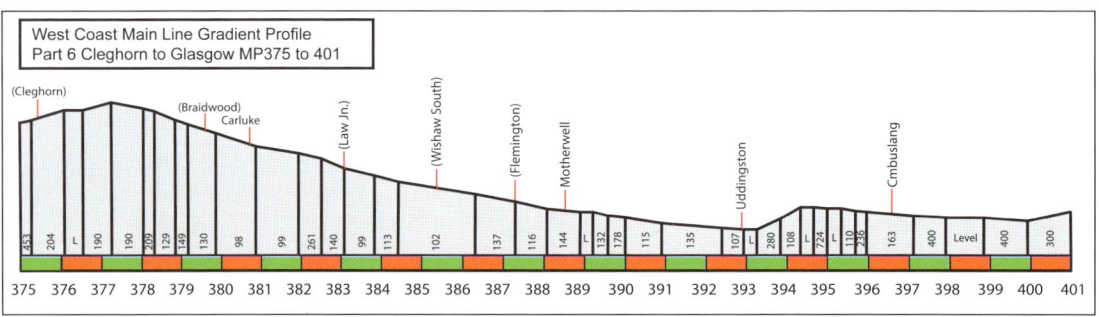

entrance and exit to Glasgow Central include a complex system of crossing trackwork, necessitating a slow approach and departure. In the 1980s, following a derailment, 1Co-Co-1 diesels (Classes 40, 45 and 46) were banned from Glasgow Central station because of this trackwork.

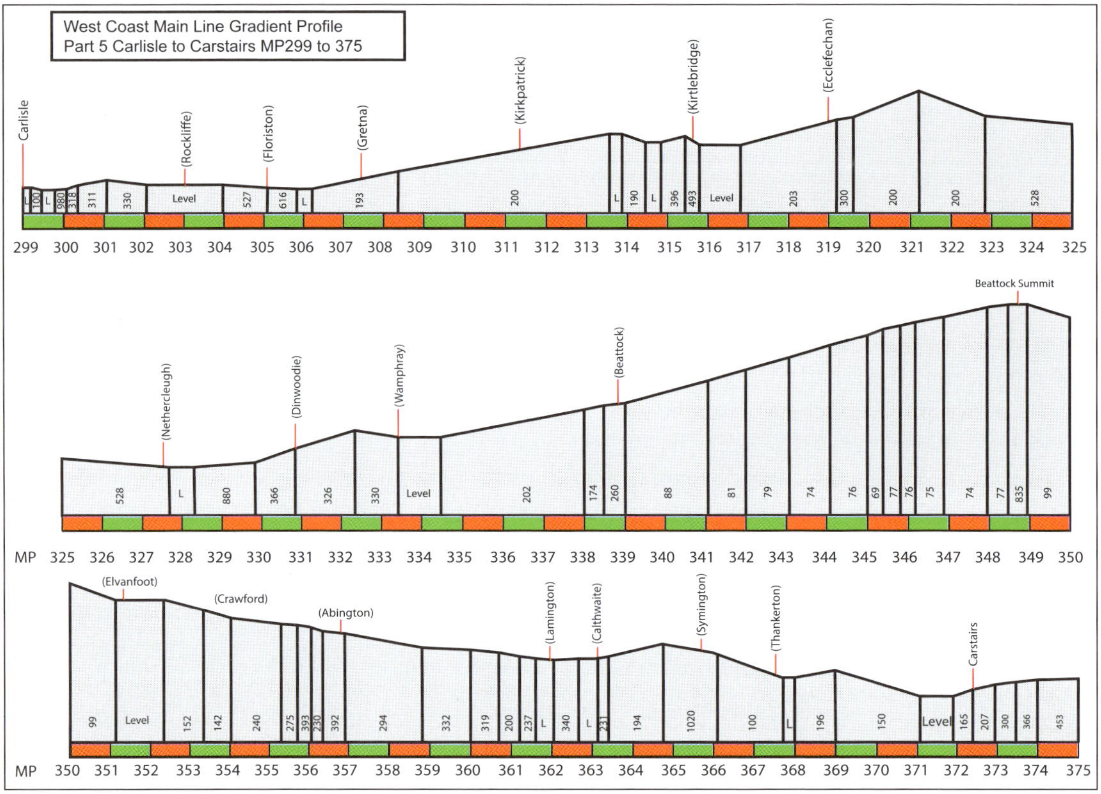

Mileposts

The numbering sequences for mileposts are complex. The LNWR provided one series from Euston to Golborne Junction (north of Warrington) with a fresh series north to Preston from this point. Another two sequences were started at Preston, then Lancaster northwards and another series put in place from Carlisle to Glasgow and Edinburgh by the Caledonian Railway.

Some original mileposts are still in place, although they have been either superseded or replaced by BR concrete or glass-fibre examples, all on the down (west) side of the line.

Chapter 2
Service Development

From its earliest days, the route was one of the busiest in the country. An extract departure board for express services from Euston in 1887 includes:

- 09.30 Wolverhampton
- 10.00 Scotch express
- 10.10 Liverpool/Manchester express
- 10.15 Bletchley stopper
- 10.30 North Wales/Lake District express
- 11.00 North express (with portions for Aberdeen, Inverness, Edinburgh and Glasgow)

Departure patterns and timings remained fairly static between the 1880s and 1930s, when more powerful locomotives were introduced by the LMS. In 1924, LMS 'Compounds' began appearing on Euston–Manchester services via Stoke and/or Crewe, these sharing duties with ex-LNWR 4-6-0 classes.

Taken from an official LNWR postcard issued in 1905, 'Jubilee' Class 4-4-0 Webb 'Compound' 1914 is seen at Rugby on a Manchester to Euston express in November 1904. The complex history of LNWR steam locos is amply displayed with this 40-strong class. Built at Crewe in 1899, then later rebuilt as a two-cylinder simple 'Renown' class loco in 1916 under George Whale, the loco was later renumbered from 1914 to 1257, then finally as 5144 under the LMS. Another class of four-cylinder Webb 'Compounds', the 'Alfred the Greats' were also rebuilt as 'Renowns'. The rebuilds were all withdrawn by the LMS by 1931, with none passing into preservation. (Andy Flowers Collection)

92033 is ready for the off at Glasgow Central on 15 May 2015 with the 'Lowlander' sleeper, the 1C16 23.40 to London Euston. At this stage, the services were still utilising Mk.3 sleeper coaches with Mk.2 'day' coaches. Class 92s are now the last remaining locomotives hauling scheduled passenger services on the WCML, with Mk.5 stock used on all sleeper services.

The Royal Train is no stranger to the West Coast Main Line, being based at Wolverton. Here the stock is being returned empty to its home base on 8 February 2000, hauled by Class 47 47799 *Prince Henry*. Today, the dedicated locos for this train are Class 67s, 67005 and 67006. (Andy Flowers Collection)

All pre-grouping types were replaced from the 1930s by 'Patriots' and 'Royal Scots'. From the grouping, motive power for the prestige 'Mid-Day Scot' was Lancashire & Yorkshire-designed Hughes 4-6-0s along with Midland and LMS 4-4-0 'Compounds', from 1927 'Royal Scots' and, from 1935, when through working began, Stanier 'Pacifics'.

Upon privatisation in the mid-1990s, Anglo-Scottish sleeper services were transferred to the ScotRail operation. Two services operate in each direction, the Lowlander from Edinburgh and Glasgow to Euston and vice versa, and the Highlander with portions for Fort William, Inverness and Aberdeen. The sleepers are sometimes diverted over the ECML at weekends because of engineering work or the occasional incident. In April 2015, the sleepers were separated from the ScotRail franchise and now run as an independent operation under Serco with, from 2019, new Mk.5 sleeping carriages and day coaches.

An often-overlooked type of loco-hauled passenger service over the WCML was Motorail, these being trains formed of passenger accommodation and car-carrying flat wagons. Motorail was introduced on the West Coast in 1955, but by the 1980s, the operation was in decline, serving Euston, Crewe, Carlisle, Perth, Kensington Olympia and Inverness with some trains using the WCML to and from the West Country, including the famous Stirling to Newton Abbot service. Motorail services ceased in 1995.

Stopping services

Some of the first LNWR locos designed for local passenger services were Webb's 0-6-2T 'Watford Tanks'. These were a tank version of the 0-6-0 'Cauliflower' tender locos and hauled the distinctive 50ft suburban coaches on Euston to Watford services. They also replaced the 2-4-0 'Samson' Class on many local and stopping services. The LNWR introduced a number of four-coupled passenger tank engines, including 4-4-0T 'Metropolitan Tanks' from 1871, later converted to 4-4-2Ts and used on suburban trains around Manchester.

Bowen Cooke introduced a series of powerful and effective 4-6-2 tanks from 1911 onwards. Apart from use on suburban passenger duties, they piloted and banked tender engines over Shap Summit. Later passenger tanks included Whale's large 4-4-2T 'Precursors', introduced in 1906 and used extensively around London, Birmingham, and Manchester, while also occasionally making piloting appearances on expresses. Another series of passenger tanks were the 2-4-2Ts, the 5ft 6in Radial Tanks/Mansion House/Prince Tanks.

The Webb Coal tanks were regarded as having insufficient braking power for unfitted goods services and were used on local stopping passenger services, particularly around Manchester and Liverpool. Webb's 'Prince of Wales' 4-6-2Ts were rated as 3P and were found on stopping services on the west coast up to the mid-1930s. The 160-strong 1P Webb 5ft 6in tanks were found all over the LMS and noted on local stopping services in the Coventry area.

By the end of Victorian times, many of the classes superseded on express duties, such as the 'Experiments', were used on stopping services. 'Precursor' and 'Prince of Wales' 4-6-2T tanks were used on local stopping services, including over the arduous northern section north of Lancaster. L&Y types were regulars on services from Manchester to Windermere, including Class 3 4-4-0s. Ex-NSR locos, such as Class M 0-4-4Ts, could be seen as far south as Rugby, working stopping services such as Walsall–Stoke trains into the mid-1930s.

2-6-4Ts, classified as 4P for output, became standard steam locos for many branch line and local stopping services on the WCML in the 20th century, beginning with designs by Fowler then two Stanier types, firstly 37 examples of a three-cylinder version in 1934 and then the following year, 206 examples of a two-cylinder type. The three-cylinder Stanier 2-6-4Ts were introduced on Watford–Euston stopping

Black 5 45114 is seen at Watford in the late 1950s, on a stopping service from London Euston to Tring or Bletchley. (Andy Flowers Collection/Through Their Eyes)

services from 1934, working for a year before being transferred to Tilbury. The later two-cylinder versions gave good service all over the LMS, including on West Coast services such as Carlisle–Oxenholme stoppers, Euston–Bletchley trains and banking and piloting duties. They were also commonly found on piloting duties with 4-6-0s and even 'Pacifics', particularly on services north of Preston.

The final design of 2-6-4Ts were 277 built by Fairburn from 1945 onwards. They found similar roles to earlier Stanier types, namely on semi-fast, regional stopping and banking, occasionally piloting larger tender locos on front line duties and very occasionally substituting on fast express work. The lower-powered Class 3P 2-6-2Ts were uncommon on West Coast passenger duties, with Fowler, and later Stanier, designs allocated widely over the LMS but more restricted to branch line duties, although they were used on empty coaching stock duties into and out of Euston.

With an elderly LMS rake of non-compartment stock forming a local service at Northampton in the early 1950s, we see Johnson 2P 4-4-0 40482 of 1900 vintage. Rebuilt by Fowler during World War One, this elderly survivor lasted with BR until 1957. (Andy Flowers Collection/Through Their Eyes)

Trent Valley stoppers featured a wide range of traction, often larger locos. Pre-World War Two, the commonest locos were Fowler 2-6-4Ts and, in the 1930s, 'Prince of Wales' 4-6-0s could occasionally be seen, having been relegated from fast services. Post-war, trains featured Stanier 3P 2-6-2Ts then larger locos, including 4MT 2-6-4Ts or Black 5s with a few 'Patriots'. Stanier Class 2 0-4-4T 41909 was one of a small fleet of light passenger tanks built in 1932 and noted on Coventry to Nuneaton locals in the 1950s. Fowler 3MT 2-6-2T 40010 could also be seen between Nuneaton and Tamworth on through workings from Coventry/Leamington branch services from 1960 onwards. Another unusual loco type to appear at Nuneaton, usually from the Coventry branch, were Ivatt Class 2 2-6-2Ts with 41226 and 41320 amongst a number of the class noted. Standard 4MT 2-6-4Ts were noted in the 1950s on some Birmingham to Rugby stoppers, also on semi-fast services from Euston to Bletchley and Rugby.

Stafford–Nuneaton local services in the 1960s utilised an exotic variety of steam locomotives, being a regular running in turn for locos outshopped from Crewe Works. Trains could feature anything from regular 2P 'Compound' 4-4-0s to Western Region-allocated 'Jubilees'. Famously, the running in turn was 'Clan' 72008 on 13 August 1954, with Nuneaton shed even sending the 'Pacific' on to Coventry on an all stations stopper before returning it north to Crewe!

The introduction of diesels and gradual upgrade of the infrastructure brought improvements through the 1950s and 1960s. Rugby locals were dieselised in 1958, except for a few peak hour workings, including the 17.50 New Street–Rugby. This was booked for a Stanier or Fairburn 2-6-4T tank loco, although some Black 5s were also noted. Also reported in 1956 was the use of ex-Midland Railway Fowler 2P 4-4-0 40646 on the 17.25 Coventry to Birmingham New Street.

Class 24s covering Tring, Bletchley and Northampton services were badly affected by the severe winter of 1962–63 with availability plummeting, leading to a return to steam on many stopping services over the southern half of the WCML. AM10 EMUs took over local services on electrified lines in the West Midlands from 2 January 1967.

Banking

In steam days, banking and use of piloting and double-heading of freight and some heavier passenger services was commonplace. On the WCML, two main areas for banking and assistance were the climbs to Shap and Beattock summits. Maximum tonnages for Carlisle services were as follows, with the class distinction and loadings taken from the appendix to the LNWR working timetable.

- Claughton – 400t
- Superheater – 350t
- Precursor/Experiment – 300t
- Renown, Benbow and Jubilee classes – 225t
- 6ft 6in and 6ft SL – 170t

Around the time of the grouping and shortly afterwards, ex-Caledonian Pickersgill 4-6-2Ts were used for banking duties at Beattock, later replaced by McIntosh LMS-built 0-4-4Ts up to the early 1960s. Fairburn Class 4 2-6-4Ts were used from the late 1950s, replacing the Caledonian 0-4-4T Class 431s (rated as LMS 2P) built specifically for the duty. BR Standard Class 4 2-6-0s took over Beattock and Shap banking duties for the last few years of steam in the mid-1960s.

After steam ended over Shap, diesels were used for banking with Class 17 'Claytons' D8501, D8510 and D8520 noted at the end of December 1967. Banking largely ceased with the end of steam, although there are photos of 'Claytons' assisting Class 50s on heavier trains. Banking locos in the form of Class 20s returned to Beattock after electrification following some freights slipping to a stand there and on Shap during the early months of electrically hauled operations.

Electrification

Francis Web proposed electrification of the WCML in 1900 and the Ministry of Transport recommended it in a report in 1931, but it was not until the 1955 Modernisation Plan that it became a serious prospect. This advocated the withdrawal of steam and electrification of major routes, with the West Coast Main Line from London to Birmingham, Liverpool and Manchester to be the first major route electrified. 25kV AC was chosen over 1500V DC as the supply voltage following successful trials in France. Full electrification was authorised in January 1961, although electric services were already running at this stage between Manchester and Crewe.

Initial electrification work began in early 1957 with track and bridge alterations on the Crewe to Manchester line. Problems for initial testing and training for the changeover to electric traction, and the need for a dedicated line, was solved by electrification of the nine-mile long Styal Loop line between Crewe and Stockport. With the main line between Crewe and Manchester being electrified, wiring up the loop allowed familiarisation with AC traction on part of the route drivers would later work on. The Styal line was opened for electric trial running on 26 October 1958 and the route via Stockport followed from 12 June 1960.

The first passenger service using 25kV AC overheads ran on 20 January 1959, when AM2 unit 201 (later Class 302 302201) was pressed into service on a Wilmslow to Mauldeth Road working after the failure of a DMU. The AM2s were on loan from the London, Tilbury and Southend electrification scheme. The Liverpool to Crewe section was completed on 30 September 1961, one month ahead of schedule, with a limited electric service starting in January 1962.

The WCML electrification was gradually extended south, with Crewe to Stafford completed on 7 January 1963, Stafford to Lichfield on 22 October 1963, Lichfield–Nuneaton from 2 March 1964 and Nuneaton to Rugby on 16 November 1964. Cheadle Hulme to Macclesfield joined the electrified network on 14 June 1965 with the section southwards to Stoke-on-Trent, Stone and Colwich following from 5 December 1966.

Rugby to Euston opened to electric trains on 6 November 1965, this coinciding with the rebuilding of the London terminus. The Northampton loop joined on 22 November, but the route via Birmingham took until the following year for electrification to be completed, with Stafford to Wolverhampton opening on 18 April 1966 and Wolverhampton to Rugby on 6 December, although Coventry to Rugby opened on 25 October 1965.

During these extensions, Liverpool and Manchester services were re-engined at the southernmost electrified point, although Glasgow services continued to be diesel-hauled throughout. A new enhanced timetable was introduced from 18 April 1966 with electric haulage to Manchester, Liverpool, Crewe and Coventry. Electric services reached Birmingham on 6 December, together with Macclesfield to Stoke and Stafford.

The useful diversionary route between Stechford and Aston was electrified in 1967, the same year that BR sought authorisation to continue wiring through to Glasgow. Electrification was authorised northwards from Weaver Junction to Cleghorn Junction, where the Lanark branch leaves the main line, in April 1970. Again, sections were opened in stages with Weaver Junction to Bamfurlong from 19 March 1973, Bamfurlong to Preston on 11 June 1973, Kingmoor–Motherwell from 7 January 1974 and, finally, Preston to Carlisle on 25 March 1974. Through workings of electrics to Preston began on 28 July 1973, with re-engining to diesel moved from Crewe.

February 1974 saw the route from Garstang to Carlisle electrified and only small sections further north then remained, which were finished in April. 'Royal Scot' services passed to electric haulage from 22 April 1974 and the introduction of a full electric timetable from 6 May led to a cascade of diesels, including many Class 47s. These displaced other types with Class 25s and Class 40s, which lost many passenger duties in other areas of the country. The Euston to Glasgow journey time was reduced to five hours when electric working began, while services were also increased from five to eight.

Completion of the electrification programme from Carstairs to Edinburgh took until 1989 to achieve as part of the ECML electrification project and ended the haulage enthusiast's interest in Carstairs to Edinburgh portions of Anglo-Scottish services.

Total cost for electrification and modernisation of the WCML in the 1960s and 1970s, including improved bridge clearances and new power boxes at Carlisle, Warrington, Preston and Motherwell, was around £74m, or £725m in today's costs. The slow speed of the line north of Crewe into Scotland meant that BR still ran sleeper services from Liverpool and Manchester to Glasgow right up until electrification in 1974. The upgrade contrasts well with the more recent modernisation, with the BR programme delivered on time and within 3 per cent of its original estimate.

Virgin Trains was hopeful that after the recent WCML upgrade, due to be completed by 2002, the overall time between Glasgow and Euston could be reduced from five hours to four hours, with 40 minutes saved between London and Manchester – with full tilt, radio signalling, and 140mph running enabled. The £2bn budget for the upgrade was soon exceeded and when Railtrack was effectively nationalised in 2002 the project was downgraded with speed reduced to 125mph and conventional signalling retained. The total cost became nearer to £10bn with completion delayed until 2009.

Service patterns

Before railways, long distance travel was an expensive ordeal. In 1712, a stagecoach from London to Glasgow took 13.5 days. Better roads saw this reduced to four days by 1776 and 2.5 days by 1818. Euston opened on Thursday 20 July 1837 with three trains a day to Boxmoor, which were extended to Tring on 16 October and Denbigh Hall on 9 April 1838. The route to Birmingham opened on 17 September 1838.

The first through 'Scotch' services began in February 1848, leaving Euston at 10.00 and arriving in Glasgow the following morning at 01.40 (or Edinburgh at 01.30), a time of 13hrs and 40mins. By March 1848, the LNWR, Lancaster & Carlisle and Caledonian railways introduced simultaneous departures, leaving Euston and Glasgow at 09.00 and arriving at 22.00, a journey time of 13hrs. The West Coast Joint Stock arrangement between the LNWR and Caledonian Railway was a competitor for the rival east coast North British/NER/GNR services.

In 1888, the LNWR was in competition with the east coast (the first of several contests between the two routes) advertising a nine-hour service, although, without strict timetabling, runs were as low as seven-and-a-half hours. Corridor stock, introduced from 1893, together with better suspension, enabled higher speed running. A truce was signed with an agreed fastest time of eight-and-a-half hours, but the next race took place in 1895, this time for Aberdeen services, leading to another agreement. Speeds levelled on the core route to eight-and-a-quarter hours, which reduced by 15mins from 1 December 1900 following the ending of a meal stop and remained unchanged until the most famous speed race in 1932.

In 1897, New Street became a joint LNWR and Midland Railway station, becoming the major hub and interchange between cross-country and west coast services. By 1902, non-stop Birmingham to Euston services were introduced, timed as fast as two hours and five minutes, and reduced to two hours in 1905, although services needed double-heading using 'Precursors' to keep time. The 4-6-0 'Experiments', introduced after 1905, reduced the need for double-heading. Meanwhile, the GWR was competing for passenger traffic, advertising two-hour expresses from Paddington to Birmingham Snow Hill and using 'Saints' and 'Stars' for haulage.

'George the Fifth' and 'Prince of Wales' 4-6-0s were LNWR developments, enabling high-speed timings with greater loads. To assist in reducing journey times, slip coaches were provided for Coventry on some services. A two hours and ten minutes service from Birmingham to Broad Street for business travellers was also introduced in 1910, named the 'City-to-City Express'. The WCML was badly affected in World War One, austerity cutting back services. Near the end of the war, the only morning services to Glasgow were from St Pancras and timings were extended significantly.

Passenger traffic bounced back after the end of this war and two-hour Birmingham to London schedules restarted in 1921. The 1930s was regarded as the golden age of steam and the West Coast played its part in promoting speed and glamour. Anglo-Scottish LMS/LNER speed races led to advances in locomotive and stock design. The 'Royal Scot' was retimed for seven hours and 40 minutes, which was eventually improved to 6.5 hours with the introduction of the streamlined 'Coronation Scot' on 5 July 1937.

The LMS suffered heavily in World War Two, with many of its major centres bombed because of their industrial nature. As in World War One, the railway focused on freight to aid the war effort and passenger services took a backseat. The level of infrastructure damage led directors to abandon plans to reintroduce pre-war speeds and timings, and the streamlined 'Coronation Scot' was never run again. The crimson-lake loco livery had been abandoned for all over black with a maroon finish for coaches, and the LMS retained the black loco livery after the end of the war. By this time, Birmingham to Euston timings had deteriorated to two hours and 40 minutes, only recovering to two hours and ten minutes by 1958. In contrast, the Western Region in the 1950s was using 'King' Class 4-6-0s to restore two-hour timings between London and Birmingham via the GWR route to Snow Hill.

During electrification, many Birmingham to Euston services were cancelled, with the Snow Hill route again taking full advantage. Some Euston trains were diverted via Kenilworth in 1964 using the now closed line from Berkswell, also travelling along the Rugby to Leamington line, which had been closed to passenger services since 1959.

Electrically hauled Birmingham to Euston services began on 6 March 1967, these serving the rebuilt New Street with standard timings of two hours and 40 minutes. From 2 May 1977, the opening of Birmingham International saw some cross-country services re-routed via Coventry. Prior to this, trains ran from Leamington to Birmingham via Solihull, with inter-regional services occasionally diverted over the route via Coventry.

The 1980s saw sectorisation with the West Coast in the InterCity passenger business. In preparation for privatisation, 25 Train Operating Units were created on 31 March 1994, with InterCity West Coast Ltd as the precursor to the private Train Operating Company. The franchise was awarded to Virgin Rail Group Ltd on Sunday 9 March 1997 for 15 years. Franchise commitments by Virgin West Coast and Virgin CrossCountry promised large-scale replacement of loco-hauled coaching stock by 'Pendolino' EMUs and 'Voyager' DEMUs, a programme that would bring the curtain down on regular locomotive-hauled travel on the West Coast Main Line after almost 170 years.

From 2004, some 'Pendolinos' were used on North Wales Coast services, with haulage between Holyhead and Crewe using Class 57/3s with Dellner couplings and modified electrical systems. From 2007, Class 221 'Super Voyager' units with tilt took over in a reorganisation that included Virgin Trains taking over some former CrossCountry routes, including Birmingham to Glasgow and Edinburgh. In 2009, with a full 'Pendolino' service, the fastest runs between London and Glasgow were reduced to four hours and ten minutes, together with up to three trains per hour between Euston and Manchester with a running time as low as two hours and ten minutes.

The last regular daytime loco-hauled services over the WCML were operated by Virgin in the late 2000s and early 2010s. After considering hiring two Class 180 DMUs as cover following the loss of a 'Pendolino' set in the Grayrigg derailment on 23 February 2007, Virgin brought a Mk.3 set out of retirement. This was dubbed the 'Pretendolino', as the Mk.3s were re-liveried into Virgin Trains colours, thereby resembling 'Pendolinos', upon refurbishment at Doncaster in 2009. This set was used on a Fridays-only Euston to Crewe service via Birmingham until December 2012, which was hauled by EWS Class 90s, later changed to Freightliner locos.

During low 'Pendolino' availability, this set, also known as WB64, was additionally used during the day on mid-week Birmingham services. It was rehired for a Thursdays and Fridays-only Euston to Birmingham service (1G40, the 19.03 departure from Euston) from December 2013 with Direct Rail Services supplying a Class 90 that was sub-hired from DB Schenker. The final day for the 'Pretendolino' was 24 October 2014, with DRS-liveried 90034 at the helm.

Euston to Glasgow times	
1887	9hrs 45mins, with a 25min refreshment/comfort stop at Preston
1910	8hrs 15mins
1938	6hrs 30mins
1976	5hrs
1984	3hrs 52mins, record-breaking demonstration run with APT
2009	4hrs 10mins
2020	4hrs 29mins

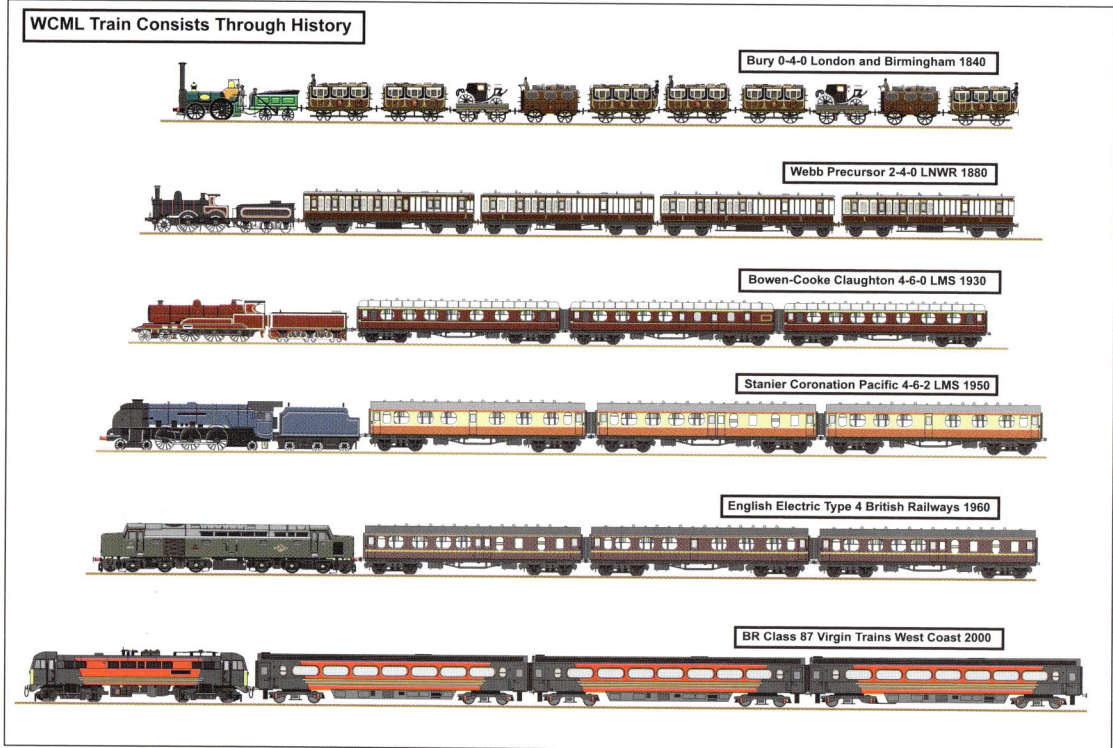

Chapter 3
Steam Traction

Over the history of the WCML, main express locos for Anglo-Scottish expresses, fast passenger locos for Birmingham, Manchester and Liverpool services and smaller locos for intermediate semi-fast and stopping services have been many and varied. Even more types were used over shorter sections where different traffic shared the route, such as cross-country services between Coventry, Birmingham and Crewe.

London and Birmingham locos

The first steam locomotives out of Euston were from contractor Edward Bury, chosen in 1836 to provide 60 2-2-0 passenger locos and 30 0-4-0 freight locos, all with inside cylinders and dome-topped fireboxes. For departures out of Euston, two stationary Camden cable engines of 60hp were built, but for the first three months of operations they were out of use, and a 'powerful engine' was hired from Robert Stephenson and Co. of Newcastle for banking. Cable working continued until July 1844, with locomotives detached from up trains at Chalk Farm and lowered into Euston at speeds not exceeding 10mph.

A close-up of the Bury loco, the earliest steam locos working out of London Euston for the London and Birmingham Railway.

LNWR locos

Like the London and Birmingham, the Grand Junction's earliest locos were built by contractors, although using six-wheeled designs, a policy adopted widely following the success of this wheel arrangement. On formation of the LNWR in 1846, the Northern, North Eastern and Southern Divisions, with works at Crewe, Longsight, and Wolverton, adopted very different motive power policies.

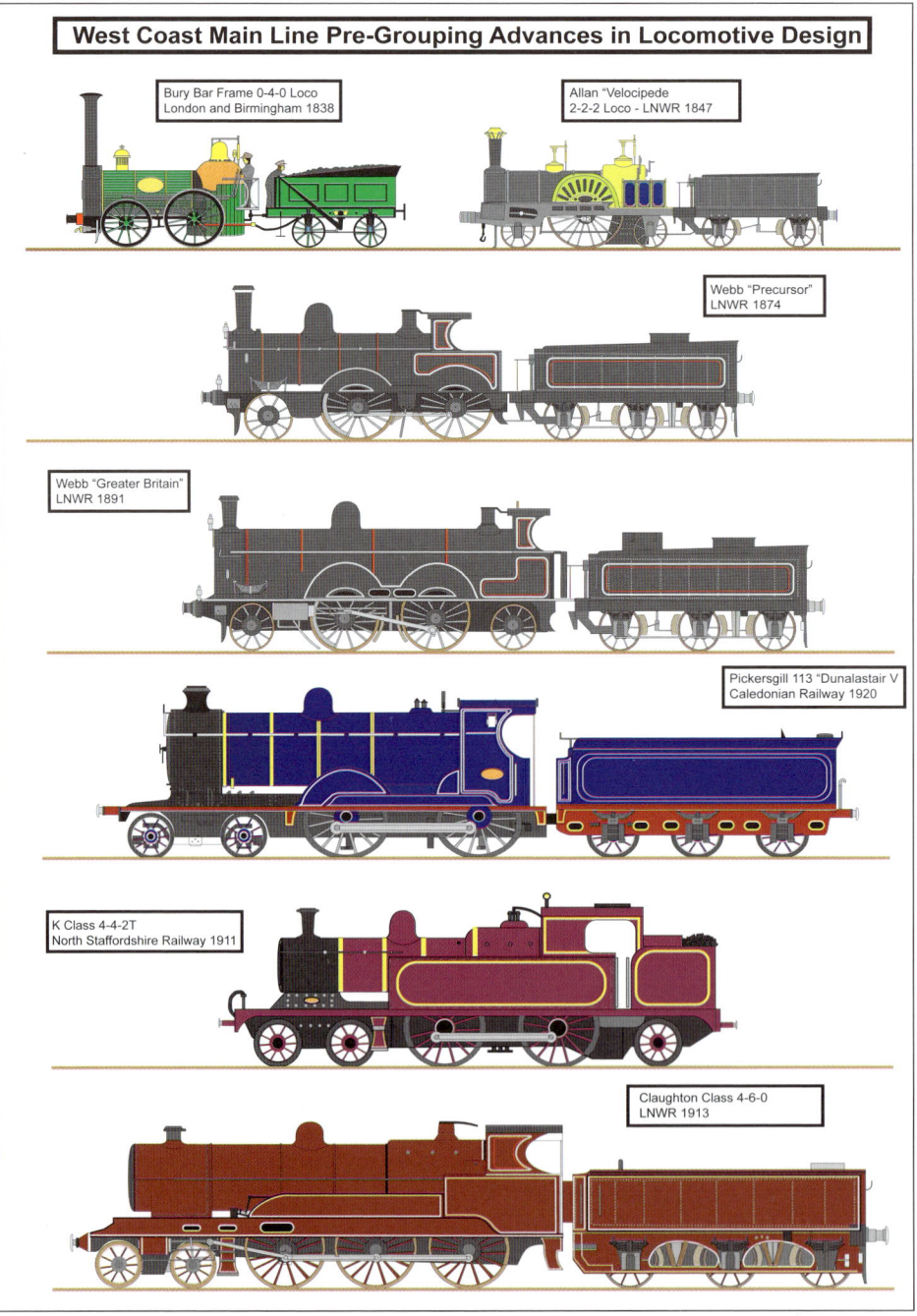

The Southern Division inherited a wide range of locos, including Bury four-wheelers, 'Sharp' Singles, 'Cramptons' and Jenny Lind 2-2-2s. Standardisation under McConnell concentrated on building larger types for faster services to Birmingham, which were distinctive in a pillar box red livery that contrasted with the green livery of Northern Division locos. McConnell 2-2-2s of 1852 were designed for two hour expresses to Birmingham at an average speed of 56mph, although it was another 50 years before this happened.

In contrast, the Northern Division inherited a standardised fleet, all 2-2-2s, and the new designs became smaller rather than larger. Introduction of the Trevithick-Allan 'singles' heralded a small engine policy, despite the Northern Division providing locos for the climbs over the Northern Fells. The so-called 'singles', with a large central driving wheel, dominated LNWR passenger loco design for decades. One example was 'Velocipede', designed and built at Crewe in 1847 by Allan for the LNWR, and one of three experimental locos, including 'Cornwall' and 'Courier', that spawned many similar designs with driving wheels between 6ft and 7ft. After several rebuilds, 'Cornwall' was still in use on front line duties up to the 1920s, being noted at Crewe on 20 July 1920 piloting 'Patriot' from Euston on the 13.15 'Corridor' for Glasgow.

LNWR Principal Main Line Passenger Locomotives

Class	Designer	Wheel Arrangement	Built	Number Built	Details
6ft Singles	Trevithick-Allan	2-2-2	1846–48 (Crewe)	47	Small firebox, crooked frames, indirect action
Velocipede	Allan	2-2-2	1847 (Crewe)	1	7ft Single
Cornwall	Trevithick	2-2-2	1847 (Crewe)	1	8ft single
Crampton types	Various	6-2-0	1847 (Crewe/Private)	3	
6ft Singles	Trevithick-Allan	2-2-2	1848–51 (Crewe)	35	Small firebox, straight frames, indirect action
6ft Singles	Trevithick-Allan	2-2-2	1851–52 (Crewe)	13	Small firebox, straight frames, direct action
6ft Singles	Trevithick-Allan	2-2-2	1853–58 (Crewe)	34	Large firebox, straight frames, direct action
7ft Singles	Trevithick-Allan	2-2-2	1854–57 (Crewe)	15	Outside frames
7ft 6in Single (Problems/Lady of the Lake Class)	Ramsbottom	2-2-2	1859–65 (Crewe)	60	Outside Cylinders, Short Wheelbase
Large Bloomers	McConnell	2-2-2	1851–62 (Various)	40	Inside frames

Class	Designer	Wheel Arrangement	Built	Number Built	Details
Small Bloomers	McConnell	2-2-2	1854–60	31	Inside frames
Extra Large Bloomers	McConnell	2-2-2	1861 (Wolverton)	3	Inside frames
Samsons	Ramsbottom/Webb	2-4-0	1863–79xxx	90	
Newtons	Ramsbottom/Webb	2-4-0	1866–73 (Crewe)	96	
Precedents	Webb	2-4-0	1874–82 (Crewe)	70	
Precursors	Webb	2-4-0	1874–79 (Crewe)	40	
Experiments	Webb	2-2-2-0	1882–84 (Crewe)	30	'Compounds'
Dreadnoughts	Webb	2-2-2-0	1884–88 (Crewe)	40	'Compounds'
Teutonics	Webb	2-2-2-0	1889–90 (Crewe)	10	'Compounds'
Whitworths (Waterloo/Small Jumbo)	Webb	2-4-0	1889–96 (Crewe)	90	
Greater Britains	Webb	2-2-2-2	1891–94 (Crewe)	10	
Rebuilt (Renewed) Precedents (Large Jumbos)	Webb	2-4-0	1893–1901 (Crewe)	158	Actually new engines
John Hick	Webb	2-2-2-2	1894–98 (Crewe)	10	
Jubilees	Webb	4-4-0	1897–1900 (Crewe)	40	'Compounds'
Alfred The Great	Webb	4-4-0	1901–03 (Crewe)	40	'Compounds'
1400 ('Bill Baileys')	Webb	4-6-0	1903–05 (Crewe)	30	Mixed Traffic 'Compounds'
Precursors	Whale	4-4-0	1904–07 (Crewe)	130	
Experiments	Whale	4-6-0	1905–10 (Crewe)	105	
Renown	Whale	4-4-0	1908–24 (Crewe)	70	2-cylinder simple rebuilds of Webb 'Compounds'
George The Fifth	Bowen Cooke	4-4-0	1910–15 (Crewe)	90	Superheated
Prince of Wales	Bowen Cooke	4-6-0	1911–24 (Various)	245	
Claughtons	Bowen Cooke	4-6-0	1913–21 (Crewe)	130	

The LNWR's first maintenance workshops were built at Wolverton, although the plant gradually moved its main work over to the carriage and wagon business. The Grand Junction began to build its own locomotive designs at Crewe, a pattern followed later by the LNWR and continuing thereafter for generations of WCML passenger locomotives, right up to the BR Class 90 electrics. The LNWR also initially produced locomotives at Wolverton, famously the McConnell 2-2-2 'Bloomers'. Loco production was centralised at Crewe from 1862. Another notable early design was Ramsbottom's 'Lady of The Lake' 2-2-2s, produced from 1862 onwards and lasting until 1907. Ramsbottom is also credited with the introduction of the world's first water troughs and scoops, designed to remove the need for time consuming watering stops.

When Ramsbottom took over control for locomotive design for the whole of the LNWR's main line in 1861, the policy of building smaller locos continued, and this was perpetuated under Webb from 1870. While the LNWR was still split into two divisions, the motive power was sectorised as follows:

Southern Division (McConnell locos)
Large 'Bloomers' 2-2-2s, for expresses.

Small 'Bloomers' 2-2-2s, for secondary services.

Extra Large 'Bloomers' 2-2-2s, large driving wheel express locos.

Northern Division (Ramsbottom locos)
'Problem'/'Lady of The Lake' Class 2-2-2s, for expresses.

'Newton' Class 2-4-0s, for Crewe-Carlisle services.

'Samson' Class 2-4-0s, for secondary services.

Upon Ramsbottom's retirement in 1871, the LNWR's Chief Mechanical Engineer post went to F.W. Webb, who introduced many successful Crewe-built designs including the 2-4-0 'Precedents'. Upon the amalgamation of the two divisions under Webb, a new series of locos were produced:

'Precedents' 2-4-0s for easily graded southern area main line expresses, which were later found to be capable of hill climbing and highly successful.

'Precursors' 2-4-0s for the northern graded route expresses.

'Whitworths' 2-4-0s for lighter duties.

'Hardwicke', one member of the 70-strong 'Precedent' class, famously covered Crewe to Carlisle at an average speed of 67.2mph in 1895, which were spectacular timings for the late Victorian age. Webb went on to develop many 7ft 'Compound' locos, including the 'Teutonics' and 2-2-2-2 'Greater Britains' along with the 2-2-2-0 three-cylinder 'Dreadnoughts', although his 'Compounds' gained a poor reputation for steaming. Principal express locos of the LNWR included:

Webb three-cylinder 'Compound' 2-2-2-2s 1890s.

Three-cylinder Webb 'Compounds' 'Jeanie Deans' 2-2-2-0s 1890s.

'Precedent' (Jumbo) 2-4-0s expresses 1880s to 1890s.

'Samson' Class 2-4-0s.

'Greater Britain' Class 2-2-2-2s.

Ramsbottom Singles/'Problem' Class (Lady of the Lake) 2-2-2s.

Webb 'Jubilee' Class 'Compound' 4-4-0s.

'Prince of Wales' 4-6-0s.

'Experiment' Class 4-6-0s.

'Precursor' 4-4-0s, later rebuilt with superheaters to bring them up to the performance levels of the 'George V' class.

Ramsbottom 'Newton' Class 2-4-0s, later rebuilt as 'Precedents'. They saw some use on piloting duties but those surviving into LMS days were relegated to branch and secondary services.

'George V' Class 4-4-0s, which were highly successful and displayed some revolutionary performances.

A total of 310 of Webb's 0-6-0 'Cauliflower' goods locos were built and they could occasionally be found on passenger duties, particularly local and stopping services. In World War One, 95 of the fleet were allocated for 'Government Traffic', which was the domestic equivalent of the overseas Railway Operating Division. The locos were used on munition and troop trains over the West Coast, while 101 of the class remained in service in 1945.

It was thought that Webb's motive power policy in the 1890s would be to use his two very similar 2-2-2-2 designs in conjunction, with the larger-wheeled 7ft 1in 'Greater Britains' south of Crewe and the 6ft 3in 'John Hicks' northwards. In the event, there was no geographical distinction with the 'John Hicks' type instead used more on the heavier secondary services and semi-fast trains. In the early 1900s, the LNWR suffered a motive power crisis due to disappointing performances by some of the new locos, particularly the 'Jubilee' 4-4-0s, so double heading became the norm for many expresses. The 'Alfred the Great' 4-4-0s, introduced from 1901 onwards, were more successful.

When Whale took over as Chief Mechanical Engineer for the LNWR in 1903, he introduced powerful locomotives that were capable of improving services. One of Whale's first acts was to withdraw the Webb 2-2-2-0 'Compounds' and replace them with his new 4-6-0 'Experiments'. Whale effectively transformed the LNWR loco fleet as the Webb three-cylinder 'Compounds' were withdrawn quickly and his new 'Precursors' represented a step change in loco performance. This highly successful class was renowned for being reliable and for their ability to be worked hard. They could run for long periods between workshop visits and were very efficient, using relatively little coal.

Introduction of Whale's successful 'Precursor' Class 4-4-0s, which were a development of the 'Jumbo' 2-4-0s, saw the need for double heading on many express turns reduced, with a single loco of the type generally allocated to the prestige 'Corridor' service. From 1909, Charles Bowen Cooke continued the good work of Whale, introducing a number of successful designs including the 'George V' and 'Claughton' classes.

The 'City-to-City' Broad Street expresses, introduced in 1910 from Birmingham to Broad Street and calling at Coventry, were worked by 'Renown' 4-4-0s and were light trains, loading to only four coaches. These trains ran until 1914 for the down and 1915 for the up service. Liverpool services were also tightly timed in this period, as fast as 3¾ hours, with motive power typically being a double-headed combination of a 'Lady of the Lake' 2-2-2 with a 'Jumbo' 2-4-0. In 1910, Liverpool to Manchester expresses were hauled by the successful 'Precursor' 4-4-0s, with even more powerful and reliable superheated 4-4-0 'George Vs' introduced in 1910, bringing further acceleration.

Two-hour Birmingham to Euston expresses were reintroduced in 1922 following World War One with 'George V' 4-4-0s as the common motive power, having been replaced on longer distance express work by the new 'Claughtons' and 'Prince of Wales' 4-6-0s. In late 1923, a Midland 'Compound' 4-4-0 was tried out on the two hour Birmingham service and by 1924, the services were shared between these, the 'George Vs' and superheated 'Precursors'.

Four of Bowen Cooke's 'Prince of Wales' Class locos (25648, 25673, 25752 and 25787) survived into British Railways ownership, being noted on secondary services such as the Nuneaton to Stafford stopping trains. Unfortunately, none survived to carry their BR allocated numbers of 58000–03.

The ultimate development of express locomotives by the LNWR were the 130-strong 4-6-0 'Claughton' Class introduced by Bowen Cooke in 1913. The LNWR loco fleet lasted many years with the last designs in service until around 1950 in the London area. This included 'Prince of Wales' Class 4-6-0s on Euston to Bletchley stoppers, while the 'Precursors' were used on Rugby locals until at least 1939. Further north, Webb 0-8-0s, including the 'Super Ds', survived even longer in freight service.

Webb 2-4-0s saw use on WCML express duties into the mid-1920s, generally working double-headed, but by the end of World War Two most ex-LNWR locos had been withdrawn with only a few classes remaining. This included eight 4-4-0s based at Chester for use along the North Wales Coast (four 'Precursors' and four 'George Vs'), together with a number of the 'Prince of Wales' 4-6-0s based at Bletchley and Stafford. There were also a few Webb 0-6-2 Coal tanks and 101 0-6-0 'Cauliflowers', some of which were based at Willesden for empty stock duties at Euston with others at Stafford and Bletchley.

Caledonian locos

The Caledonian Railway built high-powered locos for gradients between Carlisle and Glasgow, particularly Beattock. The late Victorian era had seen a dramatic increase in train weights, driving locomotive innovation to produce ever more powerful types. The earliest passenger locos on the Caledonian were the Alexander Allan Crewe type 2-2-2s. A succession of locomotive superintendents were in place during Victorian times, with Conner and later Britain adopting 4-4-0 as the standard passenger loco wheel arrangement. The appointment of Dugald Drummond in 1882 saw a highly successful series of 4-4-0 locos introduced, with boiler pressures increased to up to 200lb, power outputs up to 940hp and speeds of up to 82mph, all of which was unprecedented performance at the time.

After a number of short-term appointments, Lambie took charge in 1891, developing Drummond's ideas further before John Farquharson McIntosh took over as Chief Locomotive, Carriage and Wagon Superintendent in 1895, introducing the 4-4-0 'Dunalastairs', which again built on Drummond's designs and employed a larger boiler and firebox. The first McIntosh 4-6-0 locos were 49 and 50, these being built for heavier West Coast traffic in 1903 and, at the time, they were the most powerful locomotives in Britain.

McIntosh's most famous locomotives were introduced from 1903, starting with the 4-6-0 'Cardean', the first of a class of five locos based on 49 and 50. All five locomotives provided excellent work up until and after the grouping of 1923. 'Cardean' was exchanged with a LNWR 'Experiment' Class in 1909 and impressed with its performance, hauling trains up Shap southbound at 44mph with a trailing load of 390 tons and output of up to 1500hp.

John F McIntosh's 721 'Dunalastair' Class of 4-4-0s was a successful design that was adopted by the LMS, with some surviving into British Railways ownership in 1948. Four other types were produced, the 766, 900 and 140 classes, which all delivered reliable service. McIntosh's four series of 'Dunalastair' locos were all built in batches of 15 locos with 6ft 6in driving wheels, with each type being a slight improvement on the previous version. These were highly successful and remained in service under British Railways into the 1950s.

Caledonian Railway Principal West Coast Main Line Passenger Locomotives

Class	Designer	Wheel Arrangement	Built	Number Built	Withdrawn
8ft 2in Single	Conner	2-2-2	1859–65 (St Rollox)	12	1895
6ft 2in	Conner	2-4-0	1858–78 (various)	261	Various
7ft 2in. 'Dundee Bogies'	Brittain	4-4-0	1877	5	1912
Lambie 13 Class	Lambie	4-4-0	1894 (St Rollox)	6	1930
Dunalastair I (721 Class)	Drummond	4-4-0	1896	15	1935
Dunalastair II ('Breadalbane'/Class 766)	McIntosh	4-4-0	1897	15	1947
Dunalastair III (900 Class)	McIntosh	4-4-0	1899–1900	16	1948
Dunalastair IV (Class 140)	McIntosh	4-4-0	1904–10	19	1958
49 Class	McIntosh	4-6-0	1903	2	1933
903 Class ('Cardeans')	McIntosh	4-6-0	1906	5	1930
908 Class	McIntosh	4-6-0	1906	10	1935
139	McIntosh	4-4-0	1910 (St Rollox)	22	1957
72/113 Class (Dunalistair V)	Pickersgill	4-4-0	1916–22	48	1962
Class 60	Pickersgill	4-6-0	1915–16	6	1953
Class 72	Pickersgill	4-4-0	1920 (St Rollox)	10	1962
956 Class	Pickersgill	4-6-0	1921	4	1936

In pre-grouping days, Carlisle was the border between the LNWR and the Caledonian railways with all locomotives swapped over on Anglo-Scottish services. Until mid-Victorian times, customs formalities were carried out with levies on whisky being imported into England. The later Pickersgill designs for the Caledonian Railway, though less successful in terms of performance, proved reliable in service and some types lasted into BR service.

In 1925, the LMS held comparative tests of its inherited motive power using a dynamometer car between Preston and Carlisle. Participating locomotive types comprised a LNWR 'Claughton' 4-6-0, LNWR 'Prince of Wales' 4-6-0, a L&Y Hughes 4-6-0 N1 Class and a Midland 'Compound' 4-4-0. Later in the same year, Rollox Works (Glasgow) outshopped Pickersgill-designed Class 60 4-6-0s and from this batch, 14360 was tested on similar loads (350t) over the same route for further evaluation. The Caledonian loco performed well on the uphill stretches but was sluggish downhill and on the level.

The Hughes N1 4-6-0 proved to be the best performer, giving the fastest times in both directions, although it was also the heaviest user of coal. Hughes 4-6-0s went on to be used by the LMS on expresses, particularly over the northern sections of the WCML, although they did venture into

Euston. In service, they were often piloted by an ex-LNWR loco such as 'Claughtons'. Ex-LNWR drivers were said to prefer the Horwich L&Y types to their own Crewe-built locos. Following the tests, ex-Midland 4-4-0s were declared the best overall performers with greater efficiency of coal and water use. They took over many express passenger turns on the West Coast's northern stretch, with the ex-Caledonian locos relegated to secondary work.

Glasgow and South Western Railway locos ran over the West Coast route between Carlisle and Gretna with many different types used in pre-grouping days and a few years after the formation of the LMS, including Manson Class 128 and Class 381 4-6-0s. Carlisle in pre-grouping days was interesting for rail enthusiasts, it handling trains from seven different railway companies, including the Caledonian, LNWR, G&SW, Midland Railway (with its London St Pancras trains via the Settle and Carlisle line), North British (with trains from Edinburgh via the Waverley route), North Eastern Railway (trains from Newcastle) and the smallest company, the Maryport and Carlisle Railway.

NSR locos

The North Staffordshire section of the West Coast Main Line was built primarily for freight traffic, being curvaceous and graded. Even after the LNWR began routing some Manchester services between Macclesfield and Colwich from the 1880s onwards, the NSR still regarded the Derby to Crewe route as its main line and allocated tank engines to the Euston expresses, often a 4-4-2T, with occasional appearances by 0-6-2Ts, 4-4-0Ts or 0-6-0Ts and, after 1916, F Class 0-6-4Ts. The company had some larger tender locos, such as G Class 4-4-0s, but restricted their use to heavier expresses running to the North Wales Coast.

The NSR used tank engines for the London expresses even though they were subject to a penalty of £1 for every minute of time lost to an LNWR service working over its system. Trains, often loaded to 12 coaches, were worked by a NSR tank to Stoke and were often banked by an 0-6-2T between Macclesfield and Moss. At Stoke, an LNWR tender loco worked the train forward to Euston.

North Staffordshire Railway Principal West Coast Main Line Passenger Locomotives

Class	Designer	Wheel Arrangement	Built	Number Built	Withdrawn	Details
Class 19-Rebuilt	TW Dodds	2-4-0	1871	1	1905	
Class E	TW Dodds	0-6-0	1871–77	22	1934	
C Class	RN Angus	2-4-0T	1874–75	5	1919	Used on some express services, mostly stopping trains
Class A	C Clare	2-4-0T	1878–81	8	1932	
B Class	C Clare	2-4-0T	1882	21	1934	Used on stopping services between Stoke and Manchester
New L Class	John H Adams	0-6-2T	1908–23	28	1937	Primarily used on freight, earlier years used on Expresses

Class	Designer	Wheel Arrangement	Built	Number Built	Withdrawn	Details
Class H	John H Adams	0-6-0	1909	4	1930	
G Class	John H Adams	4-4-0	1910	4	1933	
K Class	John H Adams	4-4-2T	1911–12	7	1935	
New F Class	JA Hookham	0-6-4T	1916–19	8	1936	
New M Class	JA Hookham	0-4-4T	1920	4	1939	Used on stopping services between Stoke and Manchester

Following the grouping in 1923, ex-LNWR 4-4-0 'compounds' replaced NSR tanks on the Euston services, followed by 'Claughton' 4-6-0s by the end of the 1920s and 'Jubilees' by the mid-1930s. Weight restrictions over Congleton's viaducts meant locos such as 'Royal Scots' could not work Euston expresses via Stoke and most trains remained routed via Crewe in LMS days. In 1946, rebuilt 'Royal Scots' took over Manchester services, aided in later years by 'Britannias'.

Dieselisation came to the 'Knotty' (the common nickname for the North Staffordshire Railway and derived from the county symbol, the Staffordshire Knot) in 1958, with DMUs working between Stoke and Manchester and, prior to electrification in the 1960s, south to Rugby via Birmingham. Following electrification, the North Staffordshire route began to see more regular direct services from Euston. Extensive work included a 2.5-mile section of new main line, the Harecastle diversion, opening in 1966, built to avoid three tunnels with restricted clearances that precluded the installation of overhead electrification.

LMS locos

The grouping of 1923 saw the LMS become the largest of the 'Big Four' companies, with it inheriting 10,316 locos of 393 classes. It had been formed from 35 smaller railways, although only 12 of these had owned their own locomotives. Standardisation by 1936 saw numbers reduced to 7,691, with 173 classes, while some former companies, such as the Glasgow and South Western, had lost all of their locos.

The LMS inherited the following front line express locos from the LNWR: 104 'Experiment' 4-6-0s, 245 'Prince of Wales' 4-6-0s and 130 'Claughton' 4-6-0s. By the late 1930s, the remaining 'Precursors' had been relegated to stopping services, such as Coventry to Birmingham New Street locals.

The LMS ran in 32 of the 40 counties in England, along with large areas of Scotland and Wales and, through the Northern Counties Committee lines, in Northern Ireland as well. On formation, the new company was split into divisions based on the former companies and main lines. The WCML fell into the Western Division (containing most of the former LNWR) and the Northern Division (former Scottish routes).

Some of the L&Y George Hughes 4-6-0 (N1 Class) locos were transferred to the Western Division to displace the underpowered 'Claughtons'. However, the N1s gave little advantage over the former LNWR locos and were replaced on top link duties when the 'Royal Scot' Class locos became available. Some 'Claughtons' were rebuilt after accident damage using a larger Class G2A boiler, building on the design of the 'Royal Scots'. The experiment was successful and a programme of rebuilds took place, the new locos being initially termed 'Baby Scots' and later 'Patriots', these going on to give sterling service on semi-fast services.

'Patriot' 4551 *Lady Godiva* leaves Lancaster on an up Euston express in the early 1960s. (Andy Flowers Collection/Through Their Eyes)

Streamlined 'Coronation Pacific' 6224 *Princess Alexandra* near Tebay in a late 1930s scene, hauling a down Anglo-Scottish express. (Andy Flowers Collection/Through Their Eyes)

LMS Principal West Coast Main Line Steam Passenger Locomotives

Class	Designer	Wheel Arrangement	Built	Number Built	Withdrawn	Details
4P Compound	Fowler	4-4-0	1924–32 (Various)	195		
3P	Fowler	2-6-2T	1930–32 (Derby/Crewe)	138	1962	
6P 'Patriot'	Fowler	4-6-0	1930–34 (Crewe/Derby)	52	1964	
7P 'Royal Scot'	Fowler	4-6-0	1927–30 (Crewe/Derby)	70	1965	Rebuilt 1943–55
4MT 3-cylinder	Stanier	2-6-4T	1934 (Derby)	37	1962	
4MT 2-cylinder	Stanier	2-6-4T	1935–43 (Derby/NBL)	206	1967	
Stanier Mogul	Stanier	2-6-0	1933–34 (Crewe)	40	1966	
5MT 'Black Five'	Stanier	4-6-0	1934–51 (Various)	842	1968	
6P 'Jubilee'	Stanier	4-6-0	1934–36 (Various)	191	1967	
8P 'Princess Royal'	Stanier	4-6-2	1933–35 (Crewe)	12	1962	
8P 'Coronation Pacific'	Stanier	4-6-2	1937–48 (Crewe)	58	1964	
4MT	Fairburn	2-6-4T	1945–51 (Derby/Brighton)	277		
Ivatt Class 4	Ivatt	2-6-0	1947–52 (Various)	162		'Flying Pigs'

Comparative trials of the inherited LMS express passenger locomotives were held over the Settle and Carlisle line in 1924 to find the most efficient type to drive costs down. The WCML was also used for comparative testing purposes between Preston and Carlisle.

After the production of later, more powerful designs in the late 1920s, the 'Compounds' were relegated to lesser duties, including the Edinburgh portion of the 'Royal Scot' to and from Symington. Midland 4P 'Compound' 1054 became famous on 27 April 1928, when it hauled a relief portion of the 'Royal Scot' non-stop from London to Edinburgh, stealing a march on the LNER, which advertised its non-stop 'Flying Scotsman' service via the ECML, which was due to begin three days later.

Unfortunately, trains over the WCML remained just as heavy as pre-grouping days and the Midland 'Compounds' were not up to the task, partly because of the lack of experienced traincrew. They continued to work some expresses throughout the 1930s, particularly lighter services like the 'Lakes Express', often loaded to only six coaches, together with local stoppers between Euston and Bletchley. One of the original designs, 1033, was trialled on Euston to Wolverhampton expresses and after this successful test, the Western Division used 'Compounds' on its two-hour fast Euston to Wolverhampton expresses.

'Compounds', new and old, continued occasional appearances on express duties on the West Coast into the 1950s, even the 'Royal Scot' although usually paired with a 4-6-0. The elderly but still reliable locos were returned to front line duty on stopping services, loaded up to 11 coaches, between Northampton and Euston in the late 1950s prior to replacement of steam on these duties by Class 24 diesels.

In 1926, the LMS was loaned a GWR 'Castle' Class 4-6-0 for testing between London and Carlisle and the excellent performance led to a proposal to build 50 Castles for the West Coast, although Swindon refused to loan the drawings required for construction. Introduction of the 'Royal Scots' largely solved the LMS' need for a powerful express loco for heavy Anglo-Scottish traffic (replacing ex-Midland 4-4-0 'Compounds') but for the next tier of express workings, a replacement was needed for the 4-6-0 'Claughtons' to allow heavier loadings and accelerated services.

The LNWR tradition of rebuilding locomotives was carried on into LMS days. In 1929, authorisation was given to upgrade two 'Claughtons' with new frames and boilers. Further rebuilds were carried out between 1930 and 1934, the 52 'new' locomotives initially being termed 'Converted Claughtons' (using the boiler from 'Large Claughtons') but after the naming of 5500, this led to the name 'Patriot' being adopted for the class. To many, because they shared a chassis design with 'Royal Scots', the 'Patriots' were always known as 'Baby Scots'. The last ten 'Patriots' built at Crewe were regarded as new builds rather than conversions. 18 of the fleet were rebuilt between 1946 and 1948, the two types thereafter referred to as 'Rebuilt' and 'Un-rebuilt'.

The 'Patriots' went on to power Euston to Liverpool/Manchester services along with two-hour Euston–Birmingham expresses in the 1930s, with some duties taking them to Glasgow. The last five 'Patriots' were supplied with a Stanier taper boiler and these 'Claughton' replacements were termed 'Improved Claughtons'. After the first loco was outshopped from Crewe in 1934, the class went on to a wide variety of West Coast express services. After 5552 was named 'Silver Jubilee' in 1935, the type became known as 'Jubilees'. Both classes became collectively termed 5XPs after their power classification.

'Royal Scot' 4-6-0 46147 *The Northamptonshire Regiment* **passes Kenton (south of Harrow and Wealdstone) in July 1958 on a London Euston to Manchester service. 46147 was withdrawn from service on 1 December 1962 and cut up at Crewe the following year. (Andy Flowers Collection)**

'Jubilees' proved highly successful, being at home on express passenger and fast fitted goods services, and further orders were placed. 191 were built by 1936, becoming the most numerous of the six-coupled express passenger classes built by the 'Big Four'. 'Jubilees' saw a resurgence on expresses in the late 1940s and early 1950s while 'Patriots' and 'Scots' were being rebuilt, working Manchester and Liverpool trains. A regular turn was the 17.05 Blackpool to Euston, this returning north the following day on a Euston to Crewe semi-fast.

The LMS built a wide variety of 2-6-0 'Moguls' for lighter mixed traffic duties, although these featured less commonly on WCML passenger duties than larger tender and tank locos of Classes 4 and above, being generally restricted to freight duties. Stanier built 40 'Moguls' to his own design from 1933, these seeing use on some WCML core duties, including Glasgow to Carlisle stoppers in 1934. They also featured on services such as Birmingham–Chester and Carstairs to Edinburgh. Later LMS 'Mogul' designs included Ivatt 2MTs and 4MTs

Stanier 'Moguls' could often be found paired with BR Standard 2 2-6-0s on the summer-dated Newcastle to Blackpool services, which were routed via Stainmore and joined the West Coast at Tebay. They were also used on Manchester to Crewe stopping services prior to electrification and seasonal services to and from North Wales, which in the case of Birmingham traffic saw them traverse the WCML south of Crewe. They were rarely used on express traffic as, despite being similarly powered to a Black 5, they were never considered equivalent in terms of steam raising potential. However, one was noted working an additional service to Euston on 1 August 1963.

The Hughes/Fowler 'Crabs' were highly successful and remained to the end of steam on BR. On the West Coast, they occasionally deputised for Class 5 'Jubilees' or Black 5 and in the early 1950s, Longsight examples were regular performers on Euston expresses. They also made some appearances on Carlisle to Preston stoppers. In contrast, the Ivatt 2s were uncommon on the West Coast on passenger services, although Coventry-allocated 46446 was used on a football special from its home town to Witton on 6 September 1958. Ivatt 4s were also uncommon on West Coast passenger duties, though were noted on lighter services including Trent Valley stoppers in the late 1950s.

LMS Class 2P 4-4-0s were noted (40694 and 40565) piloting heavier expresses between Carlisle and Preston. They were also employed on Trent Valley locals, such as Coventry and Nuneaton to Stafford stoppers, and also on some Cumbrian to Manchester services into the 1950s, often paired with 2-6-4Ts of various vintages.

The first of Stanier's 'Pacifics' was produced in 1933, the 'Princess Royal' Class, beginning with 6200. The next loco off the production line was 6201 and, from then on, the type was generally referred to as

Class 8P 4-6-2 Stanier 'Pacific' 46200 *The Princess Royal* **arrives at Crewe in the summer of 1957 on a very mixed rake of stock forming a service for London Euston. The loco was withdrawn on 17 November 1962, being the last of the class in service. (Andy Flowers Collection/Through Their Eyes)**

'Duchess' 46242 *City of Glasgow* leads a short set at Elsworth, just south of Sandbach, in the late 1950s, prior to the start of electrification work on the line. The short train length and clean looking paintwork strongly indicates that the loco is on a running in turn on a Manchester–Crewe stopping service; a mundane duty for a large 'Pacific' such as this. (Andy Flowers Collection)

the 'Lizzies' The later 'Pacifics', the 'Princess Coronation' Class, were more powerful and became even more famous. Produced from 1937, and immediately becoming widely known as 'Duchesses' from the early names applied, these powerful locos went on to work top West Coast expresses right through to the end of steam on the line.

On 29 June 1937, 6220 hauled a special test run to Crewe, achieving 114mph down Madeley Bank into Crewe, thereby retrieving the speed record from the LNER, but narrowly avoiding disaster. The train was signalled into Platform 3 at Crewe with a speed restriction of 20mph and 6220 snaked across points and into the curved section at 52mph with much smashing of crockery onboard. From 1938, 'Pacifics' were allowed into Manchester London Road, often working the 10.30 service from Euston with two 'Princess Royals' allocated to Longsight from 1939. Roland Bond, former CME of British Railways, regarded the 'Duchesses' as the best Class 8 express steam loco Britain had built. He tried transferring some to the Southern Region for express workings but was unable to do this for clearance reasons.

Two experimental locomotives, the 'Turbomotive' 46202, which was a modified 'Princess Royal' built in 1935 and using turbines instead of cylinders, and BR Standard Class 8 71000 were also regular performers on the WCML. The 'Turbomotive' often appeared on the 'Red Rose' (a Euston to Liverpool Lime Street named train) and the 'Duke' was often seen on Crewe-allocated 'Pacific' turns. 'Turbomotive' was rebuilt as a conventional locomotive, 46202 'Princess Anne', and 71000 was largely restricted to the North Wales Coast, although it made it to Glasgow at least once, being noted on 21 August 1954 on a Birmingham service. 71000 was renowned as a poor steamer, but drafting modifications in preservation solved some of the issues that saw it only in service for eight years between 1954 and 1962.

By the 1950s, loco allocations for West Coast express traffic were settled with the premier trains of the day, the up and down 'Royal Scots', firmly in the hands of 'Princess Coronations'. The 'Mid-Day Scot' was often powered by a Crewe 'Princess Royal', with other locos powering prestige trains including the 'Red Rose', 'Merseyside Express', 'Manxman' and 'Shamrock'.

BR Standard steam

BR Standard types were not as prevalent on the WCML as elsewhere, the Midland Region retaining a large presence of ex-LMS types. Standard Class 4MT 4-6-0s appeared on semi-fast services and were noted for their workings on Liverpool and Manchester portions of Anglo-Scottish express services to and from Preston, along with a number of the shorter semi-fast services from Euston, notably to Tring or Bletchley. These duties also occasionally featured Standard 4 tanks.

Standard 5 4-6-0s were better regarded and would often work fast or semi-fast services with the similarly rated Black 5s. They were common on Edinburgh to Carstairs stopping trains and portions. Standard 5s were also seen on some Birmingham to Liverpool and Manchester semi-fast services in the 1950s and 1960s.

British Railways Principal Steam and Diesel Locomotives for WCML Passenger Work

Class	Wheel Arrangement	Built	Number Built	Withdrawn	Details
BR Class D16/1 'LMS Twins'	Co-Co	1947–48 (Derby)	2	1966	First British Main Line Diesels
BR Standard 2	2-6-0	1952–56 (Darlington)	65	1967	Used on a few lighter stopping trains and as pilots
BR Standard 4	4-6-0	1951–57 (Swindon)	80	1967	Generally found on lighter duties, particularly summer or excursion trains
BR Standard 5	4-6-0	1951–57 (Derby/Doncaster)	172	1968	Generally found on lighter duties, particularly Summer or excursion trains
BR Standard 6 Clan	4-6-2	1951–52 (Derby)	10	1966	Unsuccesful Class used on Northern section of WCML
BR Standard 7 Brittania	4-6-2	1951–54 (Crewe)	55	1968	Used on lighter duties compared to Stanier 'Pacifics'
BR 4MT Tank	2-6-4T	1951–56 (Various)	155	1967	Used in conjunction with LMS 2-6-4T designs
DP1 Deltic Prototype	Co-Co	1955 (English Electric, Preston)	1	1960	Succesful forerunner of Deltic Fleet for ECML

Steam Traction

Class	Wheel Arrangement	Built	Number Built	Withdrawn	Details
DP2	Co-Co	1962 (English Electric, Vulcan Foundry)	1	1967	Withdrawn after crash on ECML
Class 40	1Co-Co1	1958–62 (EE, Vulcan, RSH, Darlington)	200	1985	Early express work, later mostly freight
Class 44	1Co-Co1	1959–60 (Derby Works)	10	1980	Early express work, later mostly freight, replaced by Class 40s
Class 47	Co-Co	1962–68 (Crewe/Brush, Loughborough)	512	N/A	Used today for stock transfers
Class 50	Co-Co	1967–68 (Vulcan Foundry)	50	N/A	Used today for stock transfers
Class 57/3	Co-Co	2002–03 (Brush, Loughborough)	16	N/A	Standby 'Thunderbird' Locos

BR Standard 'Britannias' were not initially favoured on the WCML, being used largely in East Anglia and to a lesser extent on the Western Region; the LM preferring its Stanier 'Pacifics' and Class 5 fleet. The new Standards were later noted on some of the lighter expresses on the WCML and in their final years, all Britannias were allocated to the LM with some at Willesden and Crewe sheds. Services to the North West, including Barrow, became popular choices and 70031 was noted hauling the 'Lakes Express' out of Euston on 7 August 1964, just before the start of electric services.

On 1 August 1965, the view of Willesden shed sees steam still well in evidence including Black 5 4-6-0 45292, another unidentified Black 5 behind it and BR Standard Class 4 76037 in the background. (Andy Flowers Collection)

Rare steam workings

LMS steam passenger types proved reliable and successful, giving little opportunity for freight locos to appear as substitutes. This, together with the availability of versatile standby locomotives such as the Black 5s, meant there were few appearances by freight locos on the West Coast in steam days.

The 4F 0-6-0 freight type was the LMS' most numerous class, totalling 772 locos, with 192 inherited from the Midland Railway and 575 built under LMS auspices with five ex-MR locos passed on from the Somerset & Dorset in 1930. With such a large fleet, and with great longevity, it was inevitable that some 4Fs would see passenger duty, albeit still something of a rarity. They could occasionally be found on excursion traffic, particularly in the North West of England, and they saw more regular work on Broad Street to Tring locals in the 1930s.

9Fs were reported on a number of seasonal and excursion duties, although the 2-8-0 8Fs were rare indeed. However, 48122 was noted on empty stock duties at London Euston in 1958. Another rare loco used on such duties for a time at Euston in 1958 was Neasden-allocated Thompson Class L1 2-6-4T 67747. Neasden was a sub-shed of King's Cross but, on transfer to the Midland Region, came under Cricklewood.

Some exotic locos appeared on stretches of the West Coast, including ex-LNER B1s between Rugby and Birmingham on trains from Norwich, which were now running via Leicester and Nuneaton. A notable working took place on 30 August 1947, when ex-LYR 0-6-0 12336 piloted 'Jubilee' 5661 on a Glasgow to Manchester service loaded to 15 coaches. Another rare appearance was on 9 August 1951, when former LNER B1 61353 piloted 'Duchess' 46236 from Rugby on the 10.40 Euston to Carlisle, this working back to its home depot of Keith after trials at the Rugby Test Centre.

Ex-LNER A1 'Pacifics' worked over the northern section of the WCML in the early 1950s after some were allocated to Polmadie. One turn was an up postal to Crewe, returning north on a Birmingham to Glasgow passenger service. In the 1960s, A2/A3s and A4s 60012 and 60161 were allocated to Polmadie for a while to take over duties formerly carried out by 'Coronation Pacifics' and were noted working between Glasgow and Carlisle. The A4s were also seen on sleeper services as far as Carlisle. Further A4s were later allocated to Polmadie (60152 and 60159–61), working as far south as Crewe.

One highly unusual passenger appearance, albeit a railtour over only a short section of the WCML, was former LWR Ramsbottom/Webb 0-6-0T carriage department shunter CD7 on 28 June 1958 on a special between Wolverton Works and Newport Pagnell. Exotic eastern motive power could be seen in the northwest, beginning with North Eastern Railway 174 Class 0-6-0s on excursions from the North East to Windermere in late Victorian times and latterly LNER types including B1s and the 'Pacific' A1s to A4s. More ex-LNER types appeared at Carlisle in later years on Newcastle services including V2s on trains to Stranraer along with B1s, B16s, A3s and A4s.

At Willesden Junction, a number of Southern visitors could be seen on inter-regional and excursion traffic. Even up to the 1950s, pre-grouping Southern locos appeared including LBSCR types with, in August 1956, ex-LBSCR 4-4-2 32424, noted on a Saturdays-only Hastings to Leicester service. West Country 'Pacific' 34010 was noted on a football excursion to Wembley in 1959.

The end of steam

During large scale dieselisation in the 1960s, steam prevailed over much of the London Midland Region. Availability of Type 4 diesels from the 1960s onwards saw 'Pacifics' begin to make appearances on Wolverhampton to Euston trains after New Street was cleared for their use and steam persisted on some Birmingham and Coventry express services right up until 1963.

By 1962, Class 24s transferred from the Southern Region saw Rugby lose its allocation of 'un-rebuilt Patriots' used on locals, though steam returned in the bad winter of 1962 to cover for unavailable diesels. Loco types used proved interesting for local enthusiasts with 'Royal Scots', Stanier 2-6-0s and even some 'Pacifics'.

Despite the concentration of available steam in the Preston area, Class 5s and 'Britannias' were still occasionally seen north of Carlisle on services right up to 1967. The Shap and Tebay area became a draw for photographers in the last years of steam, with the last locos still seeing use on a variety of freight and secondary passenger services. The beginning of 1968 saw around 350 steam locomotives still operable, concentrated in the Liverpool, Manchester and Carnforth triangle with nine passenger diagrams travelling along or near to the WCML.

1968 saw the end of timetabled steam on main line railways. The last timetabled steam was on 3 August 1968 when Black 5 45318 hauled the 21.25 Preston to Liverpool Exchange, this being a portion from a combined Glasgow, Manchester and Liverpool service. Shortly after, classmate 45212 left at 20.50 for Blackpool South.

Near the end of steam even the humblest of trains, including fitted freights such as this southbound service leaving Carlisle and headed by Black 5 44671, were heavily photographed. (Andy Flowers Collection/Through Their Eyes)

Chapter 4
Diesel Prototypes

With challenging gradients and high-speed running over certain sections, the WCML has been a test site for many diesel and electric prototypes over the years. As a main line passing through many of the country's major industrial areas, it was also used to test smaller locomotives and units near their place of manufacture.

The LMS is regarded to have introduced the first main line diesels in 1947 with the first of the LMS Co-Co 'twins', 10000 and 10001, although the LNER had received WG Armstrong Whitworth & Co 880hp 2-C-2/1Co-Co1 D9 in 1933, which was tested on LNER routes in the northeast of England, including Newcastle to Carlisle on passenger trains, thereby technically making it the first main line diesel to work over the WCML. The LMS still claimed 10000 as a first though, as the LNER never bought D9 and it remained experimental.

On 5 October 1948, the LMS 'twins' made their debut on the 13.00 Euston to Glasgow 'Mid-Day Scot'. 10000 and 10001 were noted keeping good time on the services, often arriving early on the slackly timed trains. The two locos were often coupled together to provide 3,200hp and were considered equivalent to a Class 8 'Pacific' when hauling 15 coaches, though in reality they delivered significantly better performance. After 1958, the locos found themselves relegated to outer suburban duties from Euston, including Bletchley stoppers.

English Electric initially provided travelling fitters, ensuring the new locos remained in service. After a few years and with more drivers trained up and adept at fault finding thanks to an extensive training programme at Derby, these fitters were able to relax on standby in London and Blackpool. The writers of the time, steam fans to a man, were highly critical. Locomotives being replaced, including Stanier 'Pacifics', were some of the most popular ever and, despite the writing being on the wall for steam, the new 'boxes' were met with anger and frustration. When analysing performance, all objectivity went out of the window when evaluating the new locos. Misgivings in the enthusiast press were not shared by traincrew and senior management, who were impressed with the performance, efficiency, comfort and reliability of the new diesels.

Singly, the 'twins' were rated as equivalent to a Class 4 2-6-4T. This appears to have been something of an underestimation of their true performance characteristics. While the largest 'Pacifics' could outperform a Class 40 on a heavy West Coast express on the long climbs to Beattock and Shap, in reality the logs from actual runs show the diesels kept similar times overall, helped by lighter loads, slacker timings (due to engineering works) and the superior acceleration of the new locos. Even the 'twins', with only 1600hp on tap, were able to top Camden Bank at 40mph with a trailing load of 500 tons, with drivers noting that the 'Pacifics' were only doing 25mph by the same stage after departure from London Euston with a similar train. 10000 was allowed 80 minutes on such loads over the 82.5 miles to Rugby with times kept and power in reserve. The 2,000hp English Electric Type 4s, which had more power and more advanced traction control, were even better.

10000 was withdrawn in December 1963 and cut up in January 1968 to the disappointment of many, while 10001 soldiered on in service until March 1966. The Ivatt Diesel Recreation Society has been formed with the intention of building a full-sized working LMS 10000. The society has secured a power unit, bogies and many other suitable spares with completion of the loco eagerly awaited.

Diesel Prototypes

The Southern Railway's experimental diesels, 10201–03, were also English Electric-derived and authorised before the LMS duo under Bulleid back in 1942. After initial trials on their home region, they ran for a time on the West Coast. Under BR, SR and LMS, 10201 and 10202 were given power classifications in line with the steam locomotive system of the time as '6P5FA', which was slightly less powerful than the locos they shared duties with on the Southern Region, the Bulleid light 'Pacifics'.

10203 entered traffic in April 1954 with a higher 2,000hp output and was used with Camden-based 10201 and 10202 on services to Glasgow, Birmingham, Liverpool and Manchester along with some local services to Bletchley and Northampton. 10203 was trialled singly on the 'Royal Scot' and appeared to have been successful. 10203 was also rated as equal to a 'Royal Scot' (Class 7) in performance terms.

Little was known in the UK about diesel traction with drivers showing concern about toxic effects of diesel fume inhalation, although advice from health authorities reassured them. The SR locos had a blunter appearance than 10000 and 10001 to fit in with the Bulleid coaching stock. The Bulleid locos were withdrawn from service at the end of 1963, well before the end of the steam locos that they were introduced to replace, although valuable lessons were learned.

10800, the forerunner of the BR Class 15s and 16s, worked a press run from Euston to Watford Junction on 14 November 1950, shortly after transferring to Willesden from Scotland. Until July 1952, 10800 worked local passenger services between Euston and Bletchley before transfer to the Southern Region. After trials on the Eastern Region, it went back to the LM, being based at Rugby from February 1955. At Rugby, 10800 worked local services to Birmingham New Street and through trains from Peterborough.

Deltic prototype DP1 first saw service on the London Midland Region in 1955, operating fast London to Liverpool freights. After withdrawal for modifications, it re-entered service with the 16.15 Euston to Liverpool 'The Shamrock' and 10.10 Liverpool to Euston 'The Merseyside Express'. It then spent a period working Euston–Carlisle services, before ending its spell on the WCML back on Liverpool trains in 1957. In its last years on the West Coast, it was allocated to a high mileage diagram

LMS 'twin' 10000 arrives at Crewe in the late 1950s on a Euston-bound service from the north. (Andy Flowers Collection)

with English Electric keen to demonstrate its reliability to secure further orders. This entailed the 00.37 Crewe–Euston, 07.55 Euston–Liverpool, 14.10 Liverpool–Euston and 19.20 Euston–Crewe.

DP1 made it to Glasgow at least once, working a Canadian trade mission charter from Euston on 3 December 1957. Despite excellent performance and levels of reliability, the LMR's chief mechanical and electrical engineer, J F Harrison, was not in favour of the design and DP1 transferred to the ECML in January 1959.

Another experimental loco seeing passenger service on the WCML was DP2, forerunner of the Class 50s. Introduced in 1962, it was tested with a 15-coach empty stock train from Crewe to Penrith on 8 May. The first timetabled turns began on 14 May, initially on Euston–Carlisle trains, then later a diagram to Blackpool. In 1965, DP2 transferred to the East Coast and was the most reliable of the Type 4 prototypes, with daily mileages of over 700. After returning to Vulcan Foundry in 1966 for amendments and fitting of electronic control equipment, DP2 returned to the WCML with another test run over Shap.

Experimental 4,000hp diesel electric HS4000 'Kestrel' was tested on Shap with a load of 24 coaches (660 tons), it breaching the summit at 46mph. It was also tested between Crewe and Nuneaton, trialling rheostatic braking for the Class 86s, with speeds of up to 102mph reached.

Also trialled on the WCML was English Electric-built gas-turbine loco GT3, which was built in 1961 and powered by kerosene; it resembled a 4-6-0 steam tender loco in appearance. With a top speed of 90mph and an output of 2,750hp, it was delivered to the test centre at Rugby. After test runs over minor lines, it was moved to Crewe for testing over Shap with long rakes of stock. The single cab design and success of the Deltic saw no further orders and it was returned to the Vulcan Foundry at the end of 1962.

Chapter 5
The Diesel Era – Type 1s

A considerable range of diesel locos have worked over the West Coast since the late 1950s on core services and inter-regional workings. Scottish Class 17s were occasionally used on excursion and local passenger trains in the summer months, particularly in the Glasgow area, and peaking in 1965. One outing was D8549 piloting Black 5 44795 on the 16.51 Glasgow Central to Gourock on 24 February 1967. Many 'Clayton' passenger workings in the Edinburgh area were over the Waverley Route, although a few were noted between Carstairs and Edinburgh (Princes Street) including D8587 on the 13.05 from Manchester on 6 August 1965. On 3 September 1965, an unidentified Class 17 was noted on the 14.05 Princes Street to Manchester with a pair on an Edinburgh to Liverpool train in 1965.

On 20 August 1958, D8018 worked the 12.18 Watford–Rugby stopper, the first recorded passenger working for the class. Rugby locos, including D8002, were noted in the early 1960s on Northampton to Birmingham locals. Class 20s appeared between Birmingham and Euston until the late 1960s, although their use became restricted to shorter trips, such as Coventry–Birmingham. The type was also

20214 and 20170 at Nuneaton, ready to drag a Manchester Piccadilly to Euston service into St Pancras following a derailment on the WCML on 21 July 1989.

Unusual diesel haulage on the WCML as 20314 and 20315 arrive at Oxenholme on the 14.10 Sundays-only Glasgow–Poole on 4 July 1999. The DRS Class 20s worked the train between Carlisle and Preston, replacing an unavailable Class 86/2. (Mike Turner)

used in the early 1960s on summer weekend excursion traffic, such as 29 May 1960 when D8041 and D8035 worked a 09.35 Hemel Hempstead to Margate charter. One notable Class 20 passenger working happened on 15 April 1965, when D8005 and D8044 worked a Euston to Liverpool relief. On 13 July 1963, the up 'Royal Scot' featured D8125 paired with D309 to Carlisle and on 5 July 1969, 8074 and 8107 worked an Edinburgh to Blackpool excursion south to at least Carlisle.

An eventful day for Class 20 haulage was 26 June 1989, the first day of the summer-dated Blythe Bridge to Blackpool and Llandudno additionals. After an earlier failure, 20065 arrived into Stoke-on-Trent and 20132+20133 took the train forward to Crewe via Stoke owing to a derailment near Kidsgrove, the '20s' possibly on the only ever working on a service train over the Stone to Norton Bridge section. Class 20s worked for the next few months with 1T08, the 09.35 Blythe Bridge–Blackpool North, and 1T09 18.42 return, this providing Class 20 haulage over the core WCML between Preston and Crewe.

The last major diversions off the WCML were on 21 July 1989 with a range of locos including 20214+20170, 20215+20108, 37213 and 56004 dragging services between Nuneaton and London St Pancras via Wigston. More rare Class 20 mileage happened on 23 September 1989 with 20020 and 20021 working 1D23, the 09.45 Wolverhampton to Llandudno via Stafford, and 1G67 17.08 return to Birmingham New Street. 27 January 1990 saw extensive engineering work between Crewe and Nuneaton with dragging over de-energised sections. The highlight was 20139 and 20160 being called upon following the failure of a Class 47, the duo working from Crewe to Nuneaton on the 14.10 Liverpool–Euston. They returned north to Crewe via Stoke-on-Trent on the 15.30 Euston–Glasgow. Class 20s also appeared on the North West gala day on 20 October 1990 between Wigan and Carnforth on Barrow trains, this featuring 20057+20140, 26025 and 31434 and 31438.

Type 2 power

Class 24s began WCML passenger duties in 1959, replacing steam on many minor workings, particularly around Euston. Some of the first workings were in early 1959 with D5015 and D5016, and later D5015, paired with D5030, on the 07.35 Holyhead to Birmingham, replacing steam at Crewe and returning next day with the 06.30 all stations Birmingham to Crewe. By 1960, regular diagrams began, including the 14.25 Rugby–Birmingham and 19.40 return. Class 24s were also noted assisting failures on top link duties, including D5016 rescuing D222 on the 'Royal Scot' on 9 October 1960, it taking the train from Watford to Bletchley with a Black 5 forward.

Class 24s took over Rugby local duties from 'Patriots' with Euston–Bletchley and Northampton stoppers also diagrammed for the type. Three of the class were used on up commuter services from Northampton and two from Bletchley on weekdays. Other notable diagrams included the 12.05 Euston–Rugby and 15.40 return. Some stopping services ran through to Birmingham and Class 24s were noted on the 19.37 Birmingham–Euston. Occasional duties further north included D5079 from Carlisle to Carstairs on the 13.05 Euston–Perth in January 1961, and on 8 August 1964, D5017 was on a mid-day Glasgow Central to Lockerbie stopper. Euston commuter Class 24s were used on excursion and charter work at weekends, including D5140 and D5146 on a Northampton to Margate special on 16 June 1962 and D5021 on a working to Hastings the same day.

From 1963, Class 24s worked some faster Euston to Birmingham services, for example on 3 August 1963, D5003 was noted at Birmingham on the 12.23 ex Watford, a train that split at Rugby with a portion going forward to Crewe. During October 1965, Rugby–Stafford locals were turned over to EMUs, enabling Class 24s to complete the replacement of steam duties on the southern WCML, Willesden closing to steam later in the month. 1966 saw the end of most Class 24 use out of Euston following electrification, with the remaining duties handed to 12 of the new Class 25s allocated to Willesden (D7660-71).

Class 25s started regular work on the WCML from 1966. On 12 August 1967, D7674 worked the 06.40 Birmingham–Glasgow forward from Carlisle, it failing at Kirkconnel and being recovered by D5055. On 5 September 1967, D7674 took over from failed Class 47 D1954 at Carlisle on the 10.25 Edinburgh–Birmingham. Transfer of more Class 25s to Carlisle saw steam use reduced in the area with all removed by the end of 1967. On 14 January 1969, a failed Class 40 was assisted by 5212 from Lancaster on a Glasgow–Birmingham service with 5291 added at Preston forward to Crewe. On 2 August 1969, BR ran a relief Morecambe–Glasgow with 5259 and 5196 and, on 28 December the same year, Class 24 5071 was provided for train heating, with Class 50 410 as pilot, on a Glasgow to Liverpool relief service as far as Carlisle.

Throughout the 1970s and early 1980s, Class 25s continued to work excursions and dragging duties on the WCML. Notably in 1980, shortages of electric locos and larger diesels led to pairs of Cricklewood Class 25s on the Kensington Olympia to Stirling Motorail service. 25180 and 25190 were noted on 2 June on the down working with 25189+25054 on the up working a day later. On 20 December 1986, 25192 worked 1B07, the 17.18 Euston–Northampton, with running noted as pleasingly loud with 12 coaches and a non-stop run to Bletchley. On the Sundays of 1 and 8 April 1984, several Class 25s were used on drags out of Euston to Milepost 6 (Willesden Power Signal Box) with 25057 noted hauling 87020 on 1S63, the 12.45 Euston–Glasgow. Other members of the class noted over the two weeks included 25209, 25218, 25236 and 25256.

In the diesel era, the Edinburgh portions of services were often worked forward from Carstairs by exotic motive power. With a journey of just over half an hour for the 27-mile trip and the train having been warmed by electric locos hauling it from the south, it was common for no-heat freight locos to work these portions, even in winter. In the 1970s, locos from Carstairs could be anything from Classes 24, 25, 26, 27, 40 or 47. By the beginning of the 1980s, even Deltics made appearances. As the 1980s progressed, Class 37s and Class 20s were common performers as main locos became Class 47/4s, the latter's train heating ability being required for the air-conditioned Mk.2 stock now common on West Coast services.

1985 was a good year for haulage on Carstairs portions with a regular relief service, the 1Z09 10.41 Exeter St Davids to Edinburgh, providing a booked working for Class 25s. This was their first since the end of the class on passenger services in Scotland in 1981. Class 25s were diagrammed to work the train after arrival on a Stanlow-Bishopbriggs oil train. On 8 July 1985, 1Z09 featured two separate pairs of Type 2s, 25266 and 25285 working the train between Crewe and Preston (diverted off the wires via Manchester) and 25089 and 25313 taking the train forward to Edinburgh from Carstairs. The relief was generally heavily loaded with up to 11 Mk.1s and the entire train ran through to Edinburgh. When '25s' did not appear, the replacement entertainment was often Class 20s with some use of Class 37s and the occasional Class 26 or 27.

One particularly rare Class 25 working happened on at least one occasion when a loco was sent light engine from Crewe to Stafford to convey a stranded passenger back home, seated in the rear cab. Class 25s still made occasional appearances on passenger trains into the mid-1980s. On 22 August 1985, 87101 failed north of Rugby on the 19.00 Euston–Holyhead and after being pushed into Nuneaton by another service, 25198 took the train to Crewe. On 30 May 1986, the failure of EMU 304013 at Ditton on a Liverpool–Crewe service saw 25901 and 25911 work to Runcorn. The last recorded working for a Class 25 on the WCML on a timetabled passenger train featured 25903 (formerly 25276) pushing 1M15, the 20.30 Inverness–Euston sleeper, from Thrimby Grange to Harrison's Sidings on 23 December 1986 after the failure of the Class 81 train loco.

Class 26s and 27s were, apart from their earliest years when they saw use on the East Coast and Midland Main Lines respectively, mostly associated with the Scottish Region. Consequently, they saw little use over the WCML, save for use on Glasgow and South Western services (traversing the West Coast between Gretna Junction and Carlisle) and on diesel-hauled portions of Anglo-Scottish services between Edinburgh Waverley and Carstairs. On rare occasions, the BRCW-built machines took passenger services further south with Class 26s reaching Preston on some additional services via the Settle and Carlisle. Class 26s were also booked for a Wednesdays-only 3P14 Carlisle to Preston parcels vans. On 2 February 1983, 27032 worked the 1V56 23.55 Glasgow Central to Bristol sleeper to Crewe after problems with the electric loco. After arrival at Carlisle, the Sulzer Type 2 was diverted via the Settle and Carlisle line, rejoining the West Coast south of Preston; rare track for a Class 27.

Class 28 Co-Bos were famous for the overnight 'Condor' freight, which was worked in pairs between London and Glasgow. On Friday and Saturday nights, the freight did not run and the Class 28s worked a fill-in passenger train, the 10.25 Glasgow to Euston as far as Carlisle, returning north on the 21.25 Euston–Glasgow sleeper. They were also seen between Carlisle and Preston, with loads of up to ten coaches over Shap. After transfer to Barrow, Co-Bos worked some Manchester services over the WCML between Carnforth and Preston.

Class 31s were rare on the WCML in earlier years but were more common after withdrawal of the Class 25s in the mid-1980s. On the Sundays of 1 and 8 April 1984, they shared dragging duties with Class 25s out of Euston. On the 1st, 31238 was noted dragging 86230 on the 10.00 to Wolverhampton with 31283 on a later departure with 86233. Other examples noted over the two weekends included 31128, 31170, 31213 and 31289. Engineering work between Preston and Lancaster on 4 March 1989 saw the welcome appearance, for haulage enthusiasts at least, of Class 31/4s on additionals between Lancaster and Carlisle, making for entertaining assaults on Shap. Locos appearing included 31413, 31430, 31441 and 31464 with Class 47 47343 also noted.

On 18 June 1989, two pairs of Class 31s were used on drags between Birmingham New Street and Wolverhampton via Aston and Bescot with 31420 and 31454 on 1G24, the 08.00 Euston–Wolverhampton, and 31290 and 31419 on 1A17, the 13.23 Wolverhampton–Euston. The following

31421 stands at Crewe in 1989 on a mixed parcels/travelling post office (TPO) overnight service for Lincoln via Derby. (Andy Flowers Collection)

Sunday saw 31284 and 31132 working 1A17 again to Birmingham New Street. In 1989 and 1991, the type were regulars on passenger trains over the WCML between Manchester, Crewe and Coventry on the 1V94 10.11 Manchester Piccadilly–Reading and 1M12 13.34 return. Lively performances ensued with 100mph recorded by the author several times approaching Crewe down Madeley Bank. 28 January 1990 saw 31407 and 31451 on the 1F26 14.59 Birmingham New Street–Liverpool Lime Street service, routed via Bescot.

Class 31s were uncommon in Scotland, particularly over the northern stretches of the West Coast, so 31412 on the 14.00 Saturdays-only Carlisle–Ayr (substituting for a non-available 37229) on 15 September 1990 was a rarity. The train, an out and back working at 10.40 from Ayr to Carlisle and 14.00 return, was booked for an Ayrshire coalfield pool Class 37 but often produced rare traction such as Class 20s and Class 26s. For example, 20122 and 20138 were used on 26 May 1990 and 26035 on 9 June the same year.

Many unusual freight locos appeared on cross-country services traversing the WCML. Perhaps one of the rarest was 37023 and 31420 on 1M79, the 16.47 Reading–Liverpool Lime Street, on 18 July 1997. On 5 July 1992, 31432 and 31442 worked the 09.45 Crewe–Blackpool North, with 37065 returning south with the 19.25 Blackpool North to Crewe the same evening. From 1992, a Fridays-only 16.45 Cardiff–Manchester Oxford Road saw Class 31s between Crewe and Manchester. This service continued with Class 37/4s until 1999. 20 June 1998 saw 31434 and 31465 on the 15.30 Bristol Temple Meads to Glasgow, working between New Street and Preston. Another Virgin CrossCountry appearance was on 30 January 1999 when 31427 worked the 15.36 Manchester Piccadilly to Birmingham International, returning north on the 18.30 to Preston. One of the last appearances of Class 31s on the West Coast was 31113 and 31308 on the 1S87 14.18 London Paddington to Glasgow on 8 February 1999. The locos were weekend engineering use only and restricted to 60mph.

Type 3 deployment

An early example of Class 33 passenger work along the WCML was on 2 January 1979, when 33002 worked a Southampton–Crewe relief throughout. Following withdrawal and run down of the Class 25 fleet, 'Cromptons' took over Crewe–Cardiff services from the summer of 1981. Some services ran through to Manchester with, usually, a Class 81 or Class 85 forward from Crewe, although Class 33s began to work throughout from early 1985. Regular Class 33 workings past Crewe began in May 1985 with the 11.15 Crewe–Bangor and 14.17 return, an extension of the 05.48 Cardiff–Crewe. During the Crewe remodelling work, this train started back at Stafford, adding more WCML mileage for the class.

33017 storms out of Coventry along the stretch of the West Coast line to Birmingham New Street on 31 August 1987, on 1Z21, the 11.17 Southampton to Carlisle control relief.

The working of 33115 throughout on 16 January 1986 on the 06.25 Poole–Manchester Piccadilly raised a few eyebrows, taking the type over rarely seen track. A regular Class 33 working in late 1985 and early 1986 was 1G00, the 04.00 Sundays-only Crewe–Birmingham New Street, with numerous diversions including Bushbury Junction, Cannock and Bescot, this taking the class over lines never seen before on passenger services. After the 1986 summer timetable, Class 33s were replaced on these services by Canton-based Class 37/4s. A final fling for the 'Cromptons' on timetabled WCML passenger duties occurred on 24 June 1987 when 33055 and 33062 worked the 06.25 Poole–Manchester Piccadilly forward from Reading through to Manchester. The locos then ran light to Liverpool, continuing the diagram with the 16.15 Liverpool–Poole.

Class 35 'Hymeks' were largely restricted to the Western Region although they made a few appearances at Birmingham New Street. The hydraulics also substituted for 'Westerns' on Paddington to Birmingham services with D7026 noted on the 06.53 from Paddington and 10.25 return on 24 November 1973 with D7028 on the 09.05 out and 12.25 back the same day.

Until the 1990s, Class 37s were uncommon on passenger duties on the WCML, although they made some appearances on scheduled trains over Shap with D6826 (later 37126, then finally 37676) noted on the summer Saturdays-only 09.00 Newcastle–Blackpool via Carlisle on 29 July 1967. On 9 July 1978, 37153 and 37237 dragged services between Glasgow and Carlisle and on 3 May 1986, 37226 appeared on a series of trains over the West Coast, comprising 1S50 07.40 Lancaster–Glasgow Central, 1M03 13.45 Glasgow Central–Carlisle and 1S88, the 17.40 Carlisle to Glasgow Central. The class worked between Crewe and Manchester from October 1987 on Cardiff trains, taking over from Classes 33 and 47.

On 27 December 1995, 37406 and 37410 both appeared on CrossCountry trains between Glasgow and Preston. 37410 started out from Glasgow on the 12.30 to Poole, it failing at Newton before rescue by 37406, this working through to Preston before returning to Glasgow on the 09.20 from Brighton. 8 August 1997 was a good day for Class 37s on CrossCountry services over the Coventry to Birmingham corridor with 37713 working 1O14, the 15.10 Liverpool Lime Street–Poole, and 37717 on 1V97, the 17.10 Manchester Piccadilly–London Paddington. On 26 May 1998, 37519 substituted for a Class 47/8 on a CrossCountry service out of Brighton and was diverted via the West Coast to Birmingham to recover time. The 16 June 1999 saw 'Heavyweight' 37898 on 1M10, the 17.10 Edinburgh Waverley–Birmingham New Street, with a lively run over Shap.

37201, with 47805 for ETH, was used on the 1O99 08.56 Birmingham New Street to Ramsgate via Wembley and return 1M79 13.48 Ramsgate–Birmingham New Street on 12 August 1995. Two years later, Virgin saw the commercial opportunities of repeating the event and on 9 August 1997, 37678

A welcome sight for any enthusiasts at Coventry on 5 August 1997 (not perhaps so welcome for any of the normal passengers) as 37372 arrives, dragging a dead 47805 on 1M05, the 06.03 London Paddington to Manchester Piccadilly. 37372 had rescued the service at Didcot and enjoyed a brisk run under the West Coast wires all the way through to Manchester, it then returning south as far as Birmingham New Street on 1V48, the 12.17 to Plymouth.

and 37417 powered the same diagram, working over the WCML via Northampton as far as Willesden before branching off to traverse London via Kensington Olympia. The Class 37s returned north back over the WCML, again as per the outwards route.

The recent use of DRS Class 37s on Northern services between Preston and Barrow saw the type, and also Class 68s, on the West Coast between Preston and Carnforth on some services. Previously Class 31s worked Manchester–Barrow services over the same stretch.

Type 4 'Whistlers' and more

Class 40s, initially allocated to the ECML and East Anglia, soon found themselves migrated to the West Coast. The LMR was happy with the Type 4s, despite their relatively low power compared to the largest 'Pacifics'. Quick acceleration away from many speed restrictions, good adhesion and reliability saw them give good performances, even on heavier expresses. Another selling point was the '40s' excellent performance on freight. By 1961, Class 40s were the main power on express WCML passenger workings, ousting Stanier 'Pacifics', and assisted by occasional workings with Class 44s. In March 1960, the Crewe–Carlisle section was used for another testing programme with D255, this having received an auxiliary generator for electric train heating. The positive results saw ETH rolled out across BR, although no other Class 40s were modified.

Even after completion of electrification, Class 40s still made occasional appearances on expresses into London. D211 hauled the 'Royal Highlander' to Euston on 14 April 1970 with D205 rescuing an electric loco at Runcorn in the same month on the 18.30 Liverpool–Euston service, dragging the train south to the capital. In their later years, Class 40s could be seen regularly on dragging duties, particularly in the north, excursion traffic and workings such as Birmingham–Llandudno summer

D230, later 40030, passes Roade (just south of Hanslope Junction, where the diversionary line to Northampton forks off to the east) on 6 August 1960 on a down express working from Euston to Liverpool. Of note are the frost protection grilles over the radiators and the nose end ladder on the cab fronts (still with full green ends). The ladders were removed in the following year. (Andy Flowers Collection)

Class 40 D376, later 40176, passes Headstone Lane in June 1962 working 'The Caledonian'. The named train, introduced on 17 June 1957, ran from Glasgow in the morning to Euston before returning to Scotland in the afternoon. It operated until 4 September 1964. (Andy Flowers Collection)

Two types of rolling stock that fall into the grey area between multiple units and loco-hauled trains are seen at Cathiron on 21 April 2020: the New Measurement Train HST on a Derby RTC to Derby RTC circular trip and a Class 325 Royal Mail EMU on a Crewe to Willesden working. The Class 325 fleet was, for a few years after 2004, hauled over the West Coast by GB Railfreight Class 87s while their motor cars were overhauled.

dated trains and Sundays-only Manchester to Birmingham workings. They could also be seen between Carlisle and Edinburgh on diverted overnight ECML sleeper services. A late return to Euston for a Class 40 on a timetabled service train happened on 28 September 1980, when 40095 arrived on the previous evening's 22.00 departure from Stranraer, working the train from Preston.

Class 42 'Warship' and Class 52 'Western' diesel hydraulics appeared occasionally through Bletchley on services from Oxford and one 'Western' made it to Crewe on an inter-regional service. Class 43 North British 'Warships' were outshedded at Bescot for a while in the late 1960s and were reported on empty stock workings between the West Midlands and Crewe.

HSTs ran over most of the WCML under BR and then various TOCs after privatisation. Britain's longest train service, the Virgin CrossCountry Aberdeen to Penzance, traversed the West Coast between Edinburgh and Birmingham New Street, while CrossCountry trains also ran to Glasgow, Liverpool and Manchester. East Coast HST services ran regularly between Carlisle and Edinburgh on diversions, these ending in 2019 when East Coast withdrew all its HSTs.

HSTs worked some WCML services from Euston, including to Holyhead, between 1991 and 2004. Virgin West Coast HSTs also worked Euston to Blackpool and some Manchester Piccadilly trains. The last WCML HST service took place on 22 May 2004 on 1H23, the 20.10 Euston–Manchester Piccadilly.

In their early years, Class 44s were used as passenger locos with duties from Euston and between St Pancras and Manchester. Initially allocated to Camden in 1959, they were loaned to Toton before returning the following year. Details of workings are sketchy but by early 1960, they had one booked train, the 07.45 Euston–Crewe, with locos also noted on Euston–Blackpool services and working to Aberdeen from Carlisle and to Glasgow by 1960. By 1961, WCML workings had been reduced, though they were still noted on a few workings, including to Manchester.

The Class 44s were transferred to Toton between February and March 1962 for freight, although D2 still appeared on the West Coast until 1964 after modifications for high-speed testing before electrification. On the Liverpool route, D2, which was re-geared and uprated to 2,500hp, attained

110mph on a three-coach load. The loco was also used on 9 August 1962 on high-speed trials between Manchester and Euston.

Class 44s and 45s outshopped from Crewe in the early 1960s were tested with a 15-coach train to Penrith. Both types along with Class 40s could also be run-in on the 07.46 Crewe–Euston, returning back to Crewe on the 'Mid-Day Scot'. Other than this, Class 45s were uncommon on the WCML but D106 appeared on the 12.25 Glasgow–Lockerbie on 2 January 1965. On 10 August 1970, Class 45 89 (later 45006) took over the Newton Abbot–Stirling Motorail service from Class 47 1670 at Carlisle.

From 1980, 1Co-Co1 locos were banned from Glasgow Central following the derailment of 45126 on 12 January. After this, services from Nottingham via the Glasgow & South West route were exclusively in the hands of Class 47s. Further south, in the last few years of the Class 45s they were regularly turned out on a morning train from Birmingham to Portsmouth via Coventry.

In July 1982, remodelling of the station throat at St Pancras saw diversions into Euston, with Saturday 3rd seeing the largest number of 'Peaks' into the terminal with a variety of Class 45/1s working services to Derby, Sheffield and Nottingham. Trains were diverted via the Bedford–Bletchley line, Leicester and Nuneaton. On 5 November 1983, 45101 was allocated for a weekend dragging duty between Preston and Crewe via Bolton, it hauling 85026 on a southbound working. Another rare turn was on 14 January 1984 when 45130 worked the 15.48 Birmingham New Street to Euston. Another drag saw 45103 haul 86212 on the 10.20 London Euston–Liverpool Lime Street on 27 May 1986.

Class 46s were the rarest of the 'Peaks' on the WCML, save for diversions of East Coast overnight services via Carlisle and Beattock. On 22 September 1972, 166 (later 46029) worked a 07.25 Glasgow Central–Euston relief through to Crewe for an electric loco forward. On 21 March 1980, 46055 worked the 12.30 Fridays-only Plymouth to Manchester Piccadilly, a train that was normally Class 47-hauled. 46009 was also noted on the train on another occasion. Pete Waterman's preserved D172 (46035) worked the 07.33 Crewe–Manchester on 19 February 2000, top and tail with 47709, this being run in connection with additional services for an event at Cardiff.

Type 4 domination

Class 47s began regular use on WCML services north of Crewe from 1966, replacing Class 40s which were relegated to freight and secondary passenger duties. BR had prioritised other main lines for the new, higher-powered Type 4s and upon the introduction of the Class 50s, they took precedence on top link duties over unelectrified portions of the West Coast. A late return to top link duties for Class 47s saw 47849 work a Wolverhampton–Euston train forward from Coventry after the failure of 87014 on 5 February 1998.

Class 47 D1949 passes Greenholm, near Tebay, on the descent from Shap Summit with an up express working to London Euston on 31 August 1967. D1949 went on to be renumbered 47506 under TOPS, then later 47707 after conversion to a push-pull fitted 100mph Class 47/7, before finally being cut up at Booth's scrapyard in Rotherham in February 2010. (Andy Flowers Collection)

47810 with 87006 pass Daw Mill Colliery in May 2004, hauled by 47828 at the other end of the train. West Coast services were seriously disrupted on this weekend with the two CrossCountry Class 47/8s hired in to top and tail a shuttle service between Nuneaton and Wolverhampton, connecting with Trent Valley services there. (Andy Flowers Collection)

Virgin repainted several of its Class 47/8 fleet into heritage colours near the end of their time in use and prior to the introduction of the 'Voyager' units. One such celebrity loco was BR Blue-liveried 47840 *North Star*, seen leaving Nuneaton on a diverted CrossCountry service from Glasgow in June 2002. After finishing with Virgin, this loco went to Cotswold Rail for a short period before being donated to the Diesel & Electric Preservation Group, which now maintains it at Williton on the West Somerset Railway.

Class 47/4 47544 departs Coventry on a Bournemouth to Manchester Piccadilly CrossCountry service in June 1985. A Class 86 will take over from Birmingham New Street for the onwards journey via Stoke under the wires.

The Diesel Era – Type 1s

The introduction of Class 50s in pairs on the 'Royal Scot' between Crewe and Glasgow from 1970 gave opportunities for an increase in speeds, and timetables were recast to take advantage of the new motive power. The up 'Royal Scot' was retimed to save 27 minutes between Carlisle and Crewe, being reduced from 148.5 minutes to 121.5. The fastest services had an average speed of an unheard of 75mph between Crewe and Carlisle. With loadings of 12 coaches, or occasionally 13, pairs of locos were needed for punctuality, although renowned train timer O S Nock noted that single Class 50s could keep time on these services, taking advantage of a generous eight minute recovery time.

Above: Class 50s made a spectacular return to Glasgow in 1988, albeit on a railtour. Here 50009 *Conqueror* and 50036 *Victorious* stand 'on the blocks' at Glasgow Central on 14 May after arriving with the 'Hoover Dambuster' from Birmingham. Shortly after the author noted the photographic possibilities of the ancient cast iron fire escape used to take this shot, he was followed by around 100 fellow passengers.

Right: 50026 arrives at Coventry on a Birmingham New Street–London Paddington service in the snow in February 1987.

When electrification work began, schedules were relaxed to allow for single line working, expanding from 121.5 minutes to 130 between Crewe and Carlisle. North of the border, daytime expresses were diverted via Dumfries from May 1971, preventing the excellent performances of the English Electric Type 4s over Beattock Bank. Disruption due to electrification and work upgrading line speeds caused delays up to 1974 when electric locomotives took over. As Class 50s could not work in multiple with other classes, when a pair was unavailable single locos were turned out or, on occasions, a Class 47; Nock again noting fine performances with 'Brush 4s' being close to keeping time on several occasions.

Nock noted excellent hill climbing with average times from Carnforth to Shap Summit as low as 22 minutes, an average speed of up to 85.7mph. With 12 coach loads, speeds were maintained at 75mph up Shap, this representing a power output of around 4,700hp for a pair of '50s'. These levels were not seen again until the introduction of the Class 87s, which were able to sustain 90mph on the same loads on Shap. Performance analysis with 409 and 413 (later 50009 and 50013) showed they had power in reserve and were not taxed on lightly timed West Coast duties.

Class 50s saw use on services over unelectrified portions of the WCML in the early 1970s from Crewe. With electrification extended through to Preston in 1973, some northbound trains were

Sadly, the sight of a diesel loco on a passenger train at Birmingham New Street is now a nostalgic scene from the past, likely to be recreated only in the event of a railtour. In happier times, 50016 *Barham* waits for the off with a London Paddington service, as a Class 304 unit stands with a stopping service for Coventry to the left.

50012 *Benbow* departs Coventry on a London Paddington to Birmingham New Street service in June 1985.

In the somewhat less than photogenic surroundings of Birmingham New Street, D9000 *Royal Scots Grey* (55022) stands after arrival on 1M79, the 17.47 from Reading to Liverpool Lime Street on 18 February 1998. The train was worked forwards from here by a Class 86/2. The sight of a Deltic on a service train anywhere on the WCML was still something of shock to many, even after several years of regular use with Virgin.

re-engined there rather than Crewe, freeing up '50s' for other duties. The first of the fleet were transferred to the Western Region in April 1974 with more reallocated on 4 May 1974, this being the start of the new electrified timetable. Just 15 Class 50s were retained on the LMR for secondary or dragging duties during engineering work before leaving for the Western Region in May 1976.

A notable working on 21 July 1986 saw 50007 work the 1S19 21.00 Bristol–Glasgow sleeper service to Carlisle, delivering it for the open day at the depot the next day. Class 50s appeared at Euston on some railtours although only one other recorded service, 50040 on a Euston to Witton football special on 25 January 1986.

'Westerns' featured on two sections of the WCML, from Coventry to Birmingham on services from Paddington, and on one notable occasion from Birmingham New Street to Crewe on an inter-regional. The class appeared regularly at Crewe, together with the Class 42 'Warships' in the days when inter-regional trains to Scotland and the northwest avoided the West Coast by travelling via Newport and Shrewsbury. On 7 August 1975 though, D1065 delighted enthusiasts by working up the Lickey Incline to Birmingham and then, amazingly, working forward to Crewe via Stafford. On 29 October 1975, D1005 was on 1V28, the 10.25 ex New Street. Issues with the usual Solihull route saw it diverted via Coventry. On another date, D1023 was reported to have been diverted via Coventry on a down service.

Deltics

Following the transfer of DP1 to the ECML, Deltics were seen occasionally on diverted trains, generally overnight services, between Newcastle and Edinburgh via Carlisle and Beattock. Appearances became regular during the Penmanshiel Tunnel reconstruction in 1979/80.

Notable appearances on the West Coast continued with D9000's use on Virgin CrossCountry services and railtours between 1997 and 2001, including on the 1S46 06.55 Birmingham New Street to Glasgow on 14 November 1997, it returning south the next day on 1V96, the 09.10 Edinburgh Waverley to Reading service as far as Birmingham New Street. Other preserved Deltics also appeared over West Coast metals on charters and railtours. On 29 November 1998, D9000 broke new ground on service trains on the West Coast when it worked the 1N41 08.45 Birmingham New Street–Preston via Stalybridge, returning south via Crewe.

Type 5 freight locos

Class 56s made infrequent outings on passenger services in the 1980s and 1990s with cross-country and dragging services diverted into Paddington. They were regular performers hauling Sunday diversions between Birmingham and Nuneaton, and occasionally to Rugby and Wolverhampton. Class 56s also worked London services from Coventry to Birmingham when overhead lines were de-energised. 56105 is reported to have rescued one WCML service, hauling it from Preston to Carlisle in the 1990s.

56042 was reported dragging between Carlisle and Penrith on 13 January 1986. The failure of 87029 at Manchester Piccadilly on 26 April 1992 on 1A32, the 13.30 to Euston, saw 56016 drag the train forward to Stafford. Another rescue job on 26 February 1994 featured 56009 taking over from 90013 at Rugby on 1X14, the 19.15 Euston–Carlisle, dragging the train through to Crewe. Some Class 56s also worked portions between Carstairs and Edinburgh Waverley, including 56124 on 30 July 1994 on the 1S77 23.50 Euston to Edinburgh and 56123 the following evening on 1S07, the 19.50 Euston to Fort William.

Above: 56032 arrives at Coventry on 5 August 1998 dragging a failed 47843 on 1S87, the 14.18 London Paddington to Glasgow.

Left: For many years, engineering work on the busy Rugby to Birmingham section of the West Coast saw Birmingham and Wolverhampton services 'dragged' by diesel locomotives between Birmingham New Street and Nuneaton, with many freight locomotives making an appearance. On 28 February 1982, 56069 is detached from a London-bound train.

Highlights of West Coast Class 56 haulage were drags that made it to Euston. 56071 starred on 21 August 1987, working into Euston after the failure of 87006 in the Rugby area. 56022 worked from Rugby into London on 18 August 1994 on 1A44, the 14.19 Wolverhampton–Euston, following the expiry of 86103.

Class 57s featured on the WCML following their introduction in the early 200s. The original passenger conversion 57601 saw extensive use on charter traffic as part of the Carnforth-based West Coast fleet. No-heat Class 57/0s converted for Freightliner use were rare on passenger trains apart from the appearance of 57003 (top and tailing with 47705) on the 07.19 Manchester–Crewe relief on 21 August 1999.

57307 *Lady Penelope* arrives at Crewe dragging a 'Pendolino' from Preston during emergency engineering work in August 2006. The regular use of Class 57/3s hauling the tilting EMUs lasted only a few years after the fitting of the required Dellner couplers. Today, DRS provides a handful of the locos as standby 'Thunderbirds' for emergency rescues.

Class 57 57313 *Tracy Island* stands at Birmingham New Street on 31 August 2008, after dragging a 'Pendolino' from London Euston on a late evening service. Regular engineering work saw Class 57/3s commonly used to drag late evening Wolverhampton–Euston and vice versa services over the de-energised WCML.

On 17 March 2003, 57303 *Alan Tracy* is posed specially at Willesden depot atop 87022 *Lew Adams The Black Prince*. At this time, the newly converted Class 57/3s were being tested with locos and stock to ascertain their likely performance in service compared to the previously used Class 47s. Initial findings proved very encouraging.

Left: 57302 *Virgil Tracy* stands at Liverpool Lime Street after dragging 87030 *Black Douglas* from Crewe on a service from London Euston on 21 December 2003.

Below: On 13 February 2005, 57312 *The Hood* is detached from an up Preston to Euston service at Crewe after dragging the set via Manchester. 87019 on the rear propelled the train forward.

Class 57/3 57308 *Tin Tin* arrives at Nuneaton on 25 September 2005 with a Birmingham to London Euston service. At the rear of the train and ready to propel the service forward to London is Network SouthEast-liveried 87012. Virgin repainted the loco in 2005 in connection with London's bid to host the 2012 Olympics, complete with 'Back the Bid London 2012' branding. Curiously, the Class 87 ended its career in Bulgaria, still resplendent in the NSE livery. The Class 57 was later transferred to Direct Rail Services.

Virgin-liveried 57301 was launched at Euston on 17 June 2002 with the 'Thunderbirds', named after the famous animated TV show. The Class 57/3s proved capable and powerful, hauling Pendolinos on test over Shap at 55mph. One unusual working was on 2 November 2005 when 57302 substituted for a 'Voyager' unit on CrossCountry's 1D94 16.24 Manchester Piccadilly–Derby service via Birmingham New Street.

With the end of 'Pendolinos' to Holyhead, greater unit reliability and reduced need for diversions following the completion of the WCML upgrade in 2008, Virgin returned the Class 57/3s to Porterbrook, the final seven going back in 2012. Today, Avanti West Coast has a handful of now DRS-operated Class 57/3s on lease and placed in strategic locations for recovering failed 'Pendolinos'.

Class 58s worked regularly, dragging AC electrics between Birmingham New Street and Nuneaton, beginning with 58004 on 1 April 1984. Occasionally, they also appeared on cross-country services between Birmingham and Coventry. The appearance of 58022 dragging 37415 on 1D64, the 08.30 Birmingham International to Bangor, as far as Crewe was a one off. Class 58s occasionally ventured further with dragging duties, including 58037 on 3 May 1988, it working the 22.10 Euston to Wolverhampton from Rugby to Coventry. Class 58s made it to London Euston on at least one occasion with 58015 working 1A18, the 06.00 from Carlisle, into the terminus on 26 February 1990. The Type 5s also worked to Paddington on several occasions on diverted services from the West Midlands, including 58032 on 27 March 1987.

Perhaps the rarest locomotive appearance on a passenger service over the WCML was on Sunday 14 May 2000 when 59206 worked 1S59, the 12.06 London Paddington to Glasgow, to Birmingham New Street. This was the first and, to date, only appearance by a Class 59 on a passenger service train, other than emergency rescues.

During the BR North West gala weekend, 60095 worked a Barrow service between Preston and Carnforth on Saturday 25 April 1992. On 26 April 1996, a '60' made it to Euston after 87018 failed between Weedon and Hanslope on the 09.31 Manchester Piccadilly to Euston. 60078 was despatched from Rugby to take the train forward. 60039 worked a Virgin CrossCountry train on 25 July 1998, the 08.52 Paddington–Manchester, following the failure of 47840 at Oxford, taking the train through to Birmingham via Coventry.

Another unusual set of circumstances saw 60015 in service on the West Coast on 2 March 1999. 87028 expired on 1D88, the 16.10 London Euston–Holyhead, at Hartshill and issues at Bescot, Oxley and Saltley prevented a suitable passenger loco being sent to rescue the service. Leicester shed instead

Class 60 60001 *The Railway Observer* stands at Birmingham International on the evening of Friday 13 July 2001 on the 'Ayr Liner' railtour. Class 60s have never been common on passenger duties and, as such, are highly prized for enthusiasts' tours such as this, despite their lack of train heat and maximum speed of only 60mph.

A very poor-quality shot, taken hurriedly hand-held, but a rare and possibly unique record of a Class 60 on a timetabled passenger service over the West Coast. On 2 March 1999, 60015 is seen at Tamworth hauling a dead 87028 *Lord President* on 1D88, the 16.10 Euston–Holyhead service. The Class 60 worked the train as far as Crewe.

provided the Class 60, it dragging the train back into Nuneaton and then forward to Crewe. In 2007, down sleepers on Sunday evenings were booked for Class 60 haulage between Crewe and Preston from September to December, although only a few appearances were made, including 60034 on 16 September with 67016 provided for ETH.

Class 66s have been less rare on timetabled WCML passenger services than other Type 5 freight diesels, despite having no ETH provision and a top speed of only 75mph. There have been appearances on timetabled service trains, beginning with 66014 working 1D63, the 09.32 Crewe–Holyhead, and 1K67, the 12.51 Holyhead–Crewe, on 2 April 1999, although these trains only touched the West Coast at Crewe. Substantial mileage for the class occurred on 25 June 1999, when 66061 dragged 87001 from Stafford to Preston via Manchester on 1S47, the 06.30 Euston–Glasgow, after the line at Winsford was blocked by a derailment. 66061 worked back south on the 1M18 07.20 Glasgow–Euston as far as Kidsgrove.

The first Class 66 haulage over the WCML, other than rescues, was 66201 on 1 June 2000, when it was sent from Millerhill to haul 1M33, the 14.40 Edinburgh to Birmingham, to Preston. While returning north light engine, it rescued 86226 on 1S87, the 14.18 Paddington–Glasgow Central, dragging it from Lockerbie through to its destination. A number of other rescues and one-off allocations of Class 66s to service trains took place by EWS with Freightliner also sending a pair, 66507 and 66519, to rescue 1G47, the 23.40 Euston–Wolverhampton, from Bletchley on 13 July 2002. An early working for a GB Railfreight Class 66/7 occurred on 2 December 2001 when 66701 worked 1G17, the 07.35 London Euston–Wolverhampton. A lack of available electric locos in the London area on 17 July 2002 saw Virgin hire 66704 for 1G35, the 16.35 Euston–Birmingham. Having a base at Willesden saw GBRf called upon several times for Class 66/7s for this service over the next few months; the only semi-regular working for the type on service trains over the WCML.

Type 5 passenger locos

Engineering work on the Chiltern line saw Wrexham and Shropshire services diverted via the WCML. In 2010, repairs to the Cefn Mawr Viaduct saw trains diverted via Chester and Crewe with Class 67s using a wide variety of alternative routes, some via Crewe and the West Midlands to Wembley, giving high-speed running over much of the West Coast. Though the 125mph locos were limited to 110mph and worked with Mk.3s, some trains saw speeds slightly above this. The author logged one '67' at 120mph (confirmed by stopwatch and GPS) on a diverted service. This may be the speed record for a diesel-hauled service on the WCML. On 27 November 2010, the only recorded working by a Class 67 on a service train over the Trent Valley line featured 67018 on a London Marylebone to Shrewsbury service diverted via Neasden Curve, Rugby, Trent Valley, Crewe and Chester.

On 17 January 2009, 67029 prepares to go 'under the wires' of the WCML as it approaches Coventry on a London Marylebone–Wrexham service. Open access company Wrexham and Shropshire operated a high-quality service, but its profitability was severely curtailed owing to being unable to call at major population centres in the West Midlands, such as Wolverhampton, Birmingham and Coventry.

An unusual sight 'on the blocks' at London Euston, with Royal train-liveried 67005 *Queen's Messenger* having arrived with the Caledonian Sleeper service from Fort William, Inverness and Aberdeen on 7 January 2009. When major engineering work take place on the West Coast, the sleeper services are often diverted via the ECML. On this day, 67005 worked the diverted service into Euston after reversal in Wembley Yard.

During the short period in the late 2010s when Northern operated loco-hauled trains around the Cumbrian Coast, some of the Class 37 and Class 68 operated services from Carlisle to Barrow-in-Furness were extended southwards over the WCML from Carnforth as far as Lancaster or Preston. On 12 September 2018, 68033 stands at Barrow with a train from Carlisle, working top and tail with 68005 *Defiant*.

DRS' Stadler/Vossloh Class 68s diesels were introduced into passenger service in 2014. WCML use has been restricted to Northern's Cumbrian Coast services, these running over the WCML between Carnforth and Preston and the short distance into Carlisle station. They have also featured on excursions and railtours and on test between Carlisle, Manchester and Bletchley with TransPennine Express Mk.5 push-pull stock.

Class 73s made it to Birmingham New Street several times on cross-country services, at least twice via Coventry. Saturday 21 August 1982 saw 73134 and 73108 achieve this with a Brighton to Manchester Piccadilly service, returning to Reading the same afternoon. On 28 January 1997, and with Virgin only three weeks into its new CrossCountry franchise, EWS loaned 73132 and 73139 to rescue a failed Class 47 at Redhill on the 14.20 Brighton–Manchester Piccadilly service, the locos working through to New Street. Up the 1 in 330 climb from Coventry to Berkswell, the '73s' managed only 40mph.

Chapter 6
Electric Locomotives

The WCML from the 1960s to the turn of the century was synonymous with AC electric locomotive haulage, though initially no AC locomotives had been built in this country. Metropolitan Vickers experimental gas turbine locomotive 18100 on the Western Region was withdrawn from service in 1958 and became a testbed 25kV electric loco, being renumbered E1000 and then E2001. The experimental loco never worked a scheduled service, although a few invited guests enjoyed haulage on a press special on 26 November 1958. By 1962, E2001 had been used to train over 1,300 drivers on AC electric traction before handing over to E3001, which was the first of the new AC types to be delivered.

Driving the new locos was very different for those trained on steam or even new diesels. Power needed to be applied gradually, through up to 38 notches, and keeping an eye on ammeters to ensure the traction motors were not overloaded; notching up as the ammeters slipped from green into red or amber. Following the delivery of the AL1s for testing, E2001 was moved to Allerton, Crewe and Stockport for testing and training. With newer locos available, it was transferred to Glasgow in 1961 for staff training in the Glasgow area before moving to Rugby test plant for static driver and fitter training. Under the new locomotive classification scheme, brought in before TOPS, E2001 was allocated the designation of Class 80. However, as it was withdrawn from stock in April 1968, it never carried its new number, which would have been 80001.

The AL1s to AL5s were ordered in the mid-1950s with delivery anticipated for 1958–60, although design issues, particularly around the electrical systems, saw the locos' delivery slightly delayed, being completed between 1959 and 1964. Production AC electric locomotives were expected to feature unpowered leading wheelsets to keep axle loadings down, but experience with Alsthom Bo-Bos on the Bern-Lötschberg-Simplon Railway and developments by SNCF in France showed advantages in an all-adhesion wheel arrangement for high-speed electric locomotives. Two of the early builds were expected to have some locos geared for 80mph for freight, and two locos were built as such, but were soon re-geared for 100mph running along with all other members of AL1 to AL5.

E3050, later 82004, runs light engine through Crewe in a scene from the early 1960s. (Andy Flowers Collection)

West Coast Main Line Electric Locomotives

Type	Builder	Original Classification	Wheel Arrangement	Output	Weight	Introduced
E2001	Metropolitan-Vickers	n/a	A1A-A1A	2,500 hp	109t	1958
81	BRCW	AL1	Bo-Bo	3,200 hp	79t	1959–60
82	Beyer Peacock	AL2	Bo-Bo	3,320 hp	78t	1960–61
83	English Electric	AL3	Bo-Bo	2,950 hp	73t	1960–61
84	NBL	AL4	Bo-Bo	3,100 hp	76t	1960
85	BREL Doncaster	AL5	Bo-Bo	3,200 hp	80t	1961–62
86	EE, Vulcan Foundry/BREL Doncaster	AL6	Bo-Bo	3,600–4,040 hp	83-87t	1965–66
87	BREL Crewe	AL7	Bo-Bo	5,000 hp	83t	1973–75
88	Stadler Rail	n/a	Bo-Bo	5,400 hp	86t	2015–16
89	Brush/BREL Crewe	n/a	Co-Co	5,850 hp	105t	1986
90	BREL Crewe	n/a	Bo-Bo	5,000 hp	85t	1987–90
92	Brush	n/a	Co-Co	6,700 hp	126t	1993–95
93	Stadler Rail	n/a	Co-Co	5,400/1,800 hp	82t?	2020–?

Manufacturers and designers were given discretion around the electrical equipment fitted, particularly rectifiers to convert overhead 25kV AC to DC for traction motors. When locomotive electronics were in their infancy, builders experimented with a range of new technologies. Different internal electrical and engineering designs of the AL1 to AL5 locos led to differences in output, reliability and performance. Class 82s had the highest rated outputs and Class 83s the lowest with Class 84s slightly lower geared, showing better performance at lower speeds. The AL1s to AL5s were delivered in a new bright shade of blue. In the early years of electrification, with many available locomotives, it was common for double-heading for balancing purposes; without multiple working,

E3068 (later 85013) stands at London Euston in a scene from the late 1960s, after arrival on a service from the north. (Andy Flowers Collection)

trailing locos were usually unpowered. The lack of ETH-capable stock saw the use of steam-heating boiler vans for a few years.

The AL1s were the first AC electrics delivered to BR for the WCML. Later classed as '81s', they were designed by British Thomson-Houston, which merged with Metropolitan Vickers to form AEI. The firm contracted construction out to BRCW with the first loco handed over in November 1959 and allocated to Longsight. Mechanically, the locos were similar to BRCW's diesels (Classes 26s, 27s and 33s). E3001 (later 81001) became the first new-build AC locomotive to be supplied to BR, being handed over at Sandbach on 27 November 1959 before beginning test running and crew training over the Styal line. The loco went into service in 1960, replacing diesel and steam at Crewe on Euston to Liverpool and Manchester services. Delivery of the Class 81s took longer than the other types, the last loco not being introduced until February 1964.

The initial allocation for the first electrics was 'AC Lines', this covering Crewe, Allerton, and Longsight, although Crewe was the main maintenance depot. The code was soon abolished with classes allocated

In January 1985, 85008 waits at Wolverhampton while working an inter-regional service to Manchester Piccadilly.

85011 stands at Carlisle in the early hours of 11 August 1990 on a down parcels service. After a short reprieve as a freight sector loco and renumbering to 85114, the AC electric was scrapped at MC Metals, Glasgow, in 1991. (Andy Flowers Collection)

to specific depots. For the Class 81s, this was Crewe before transfer to Glasgow Shields in 1975 after electrification. The type, in common with other early AC electrics, was prone to fires in later years, leading to the withdrawal of some locos. 81012 was the last of the class in main line service, being restricted to freight as an 80mph loco. The last passenger working for the class featured 81012 on the 08.47 Plymouth–Liverpool forward from Birmingham New Street on 6 April 1990. A number of Class 81s (81002 and 81004 then later 81012 and 81017) replaced the last Class 83s on Euston empty stock duties from 1989 until 1991, Class 85s then taking over. One member of the class was saved for preservation, 81002 now being located at Barrow Hill under the ownership of the AC Locomotive Group.

The AL2 order was granted to the Metropolitan Vickers division of AEI, with mechanical construction subcontracted to Beyer-Peacock Ltd of Gorton, Manchester. As parent company AEI was involved with both classes, many parts were shared with the AL1s. Bodyshells for the Class 82s were built by Beyer Peacock using a heavy, load-bearing underframe with Commonwealth-type bogies, similar to the company's 'Hymek' diesels, though lighter materials were needed to bring the loco to within weight tolerances. Unlike the '81s', '83s' and '84s', which were notoriously rough riding, the Class 82s were considered relatively smooth. Class 85s were also noted as rough riders, which was later cured by fitting of additional damping.

The first AL2 to enter service was E3046, being delivered to Longsight on 16 July 1960. The heaviest of the early types, they were allocated to Longsight for their entire main line careers. Two of the class (82005 and 82008) were moved to Willesden in 1983 for 40mph maximum speed empty stock duties around Euston with 82003 retained as a source of spares. The locos were finally withdrawn in 1987. 82008 was bought from Booths scrapyard, Rotherham, in 1993 by Pete Waterman for preservation and is now at Barrow Hill with the AC Locomotive Group.

The order for 15 AL3s was won by English Electric, these being the lightest, smallest and least powerful of the five types ordered. Initially allocated to the general pool, the class were later allocated to Longsight for the rest of their time on BR. In contrast with the Class 82s, the Class 83s came well within the specified weight requirements. E3100 was used as a successful testbed for Transductor Stepless Tap-Changer control, the rest of the class suffering major problems with their water-cooled Mercury-Arc rectifiers, as used on Classes 81-84. The loco was also considered in 1967 for testing of thyristor control and dual brake, though this was ruled out on cost grounds. Problems with the Class 83s became so severe that in 1969 the whole fleet was placed in store. Following refurbishment at Doncaster in 1973/74, during which period E3100 was returned to standard configuration, the class was returned to service to help bolster the AC fleet.

After the fleet was withdrawn in 1983, 83012 and 83015 were reallocated to stock duties at Euston, with 83009 becoming a static current converter at Longsight shed for conversion of the 25kV AC overhead supply to 1500V DC, for use while maintaining Hadfield/Glossop Class 506 EMUs. When the stub of the former Woodhead route was converted to 25kV AC operation and the Hadfield units withdrawn, 83009 joined the other survivors at Willesden. The Class 83s were replaced on these duties in 1989 and finally withdrawn. 83012 was bought for preservation by Pete Waterman and is now also based at Barrow Hill with the ACLG.

GEC won the order for ten AL4s, subcontracting the design and construction to the North British Locomotive Co. The Class 84s were tested on the electrified suburban Glasgow network before heading south to join the other early AC classes on the Manchester–Crewe line. The class used a General Electric 'Com-Pak' (Mercury Arc type) rectifier, which proved particularly unsuitable for rail use and was later changed to solid state silicon rectifiers. The Class 84s had a reputation for unreliability and poor ride quality, proving to be the most troublesome of the AC electric designs and were placed in store several times. Refurbishment in 1971/72 with new silicon rectifiers and other modifications did little to increase reliability.

85040 arrives at Wolverhampton on a Manchester Piccadilly to Birmingham New Street service in June 1985. Of note is the typical mixed coaching stock rake of the mid-1980s, including a Mk.1 buffet amongst both pressure-ventilated and air-conditioned Mk.2 stock.

As a result, Class 84s were the rarest of the early classes on passenger duties. One loco spent a day dragging a Class 304 EMU on Coventry–Birmingham stoppers in the 1970s, while a Class 84 also worked a Preston–Carlisle service as late as 1981 after the failure of a Class 87. Introduction of 110mph timings for West Coast services saw appearances by early AC locos on principal workings become even rarer. As the first of the early electrics to be earmarked for complete withdrawal, Class 84s became popular with haulage enthusiasts. 84010 hauled the somewhat premature 'Class 84 Farewell Tour' on 10 November 1979 from Manchester to Glasgow via Northampton. The fleet was finally withdrawn in 1980.

The final 40 of the initial AC electric locos, the AL5s, were built by BREL at Doncaster Works with electrical equipment similar to that in the AL1s supplied by AEI. The first loco in service was E3057 in early June 1961 with deliveries continuing until the end of 1964. After initial allocation to the general AC Lines code, the fleet moved to Longsight before being allocated to Crewe in 1973. In the late 1980s, the delayed delivery of the Class 90 fleet saw ten of the remaining Class 85s converted to freight Class 85/1s in May 1989, with the ETH isolated and maximum speed reduced to 75mph for easier maintenance, although locos were occasionally used on a number of 100mph passenger turns. For example, 85109 worked a 09.20 Glasgow–Euston relief on 19 August 1989 and the same day 85101 powered another relief, the 11.40 Glasgow–Euston.

The last booked timetabled service train for a Class 85 was 85011 on 6 October 1990 on the 'Clansman' from Euston to Carstairs, it working the up train as far as Carlisle, where it was removed with an ETH fault. The last planned passenger run with a first-series AC loco featured 85101 on the 'Roarer Requiem' on 30 June 1991, this travelling over the WCML and then some unusual locations on Great Eastern lines with 100mph running from the 75mph ageing freight loco. 85109 had the honour of the last ever unplanned appearance of an early series AC electric on a passenger working on 5 July 1991, replacing a failed 90 at Carlisle on the 05.59 Paddington to Glasgow.

'Roarer' passenger duties

In the early 1970s, a recast of the timetable saw cross-country services re-routed via Bromsgrove instead of Hereford and Shrewsbury with electric haulage north from Birmingham New Street. Concurrently, Class 81s to 85s were deemed as freight-only with very few passenger duties undertaken. With a lack of work, all of the Class 83s and Class 84s were put into store in the old steam shed at Bury. Notable workings for 'Roarers' in the 1970s included the 03.50 Euston–Hemel Hempstead, which loaded to only two parcels vans and one Mk.1 coach, and the 00.45 Crewe–Manchester, which was again only booked for three coaches.

On 22 October 1983, Class 85 85031 stands at Preston on a shortened-up service. (Andy Flowers Collection)

On 21 July 1990, 85011 prepares to take the short-formed 19.00 express to London Euston out of Manchester Piccadilly. (Clive A. Norman)

In the summer of 1986, 85020 stands at Birmingham New Street with an inter-regional service bound for Manchester Piccadilly.

Fortunes took an upturn for the early AC electrics with completion of electrification through to Glasgow. By the end of the 1970s, with increased numbers of electric locomotives in service and with BR changing its policy, allowing increased numbers of diesels to run 'under the wires', fewer AC locos were needed. The unreliable Class 84s were the first of the early AC electric fleet to be withdrawn, with all gone by the end of 1980. Classes 82 and 83 were the next to go, being withdrawn by the end of 1983, save for the few retained for Euston stock workings. In the end, the Class 81s and Class 85s were gradually withdrawn from traffic, often after failures. The remaining locomotives were prized by haulage enthusiasts in their last years in service and they are missed by many. With the preserved examples unable to work on the main line and with no electrified heritage railways, they are all now static exhibits.

Class 86s

The Class 86s built on the successful features of the AL1s to AL5s, with some new innovations. The flexible drive system was dropped in favour of conventional axle-hung traction motors, English Electric believing this would lower maintenance costs, improve ride quality and reduce production costs. Experience showed this to have been a poor decision, the high un-sprung weight from the traction motors causing bogie frame cracks and significant track damage. Fitting of Flexicoil suspension alleviated some of the issues, although the class retained a reputation for poor ride quality. The quote from one Crewe driver upon introduction into service and about to board an '86' was telling; 'Ride 'em, cowboy!'

New features of the Class 86s included rheostatic braking, Alsthom bogies, silicon rectifiers, high-tension tap changing, axle-hung traction motors and separate secondary windings on each traction motor. Other features included a single Stone-Faiveley pantograph, separate power packs for each traction motor (meaning faulty motors could be replaced more easily), a less streamlined bodyshell and higher overall output rating. The Class 86's 38-position tap changer control system was based on that in the Class 82s and proved reliable and successful in service.

With its new Flexicoil suspension, E3173 was selected for high-speed testing with one cab given a streamlined glass fibre nose; speeds of up to 129mph being recorded. The class entered service from 1965 onwards, being outshopped in an early variant of the new BR blue livery, with small yellow warning panels added after August that year. Initially, they were concentrated on passenger work with occasional freight turns.

Standard West Coast AC motive power for over 30 years, the Class 86s were largely relegated to secondary duties, such as the Euston–Birmingham circuit, by the end of the 1980s. Here, 86224 *Caledonian* approaches Canley on a Euston to Wolverhampton service in June 1986.

86614 stands at Crewe on 29 December 2006 with the 'Yo-Ho-Ho' multi-traction Christmas railtour. The Class 86/6 sub-class was rare on passenger workings and a big draw for railtour duties such as this. Freightliner inherited 30 Class 86/6s upon privatisation and they remained in traffic until 2021 when an influx of Class 90s from East Anglia allowed the veteran locos to be stood down.

The sole Class 86/5 86501 stands at Rugby on 31 May 2005 with a down container service. 86501 demonstrates the complex numbering history of some of the Class 86 fleet. Delivered as E3180 in July 1965, it was then renumbered under TOPS as 86008 in June 1973, then 86408 in November 1985 (as a 100mph-capable loco once again) before becoming a 75mph restricted Class 86/6 (86608) in October 1989. After re-gearing, it became 86501 in May 2000 before being converted back to a standard '86/6' as 86608 again in March 2016. In early 2004, the loco was reported to have worked a passenger service once again, assisting a failed Virgin service between Ledburn and Watford Junction. Its only other passenger turn as a Class 86/5 took place on 5 February 2005, working the 'East-Ender' railtour from Southend Victoria to Stratford and Wembley Yard via the North London Line.

Above: 86323 arrives at Stockport in February 1981 on a London Euston to Manchester Piccadilly service, while a Stockport to Stalybridge DMU service waits in the bay platform.

Right: The approach to Birmingham New Street is notorious for hold-ups, with drivers nicknaming Proof House Junction as 'Snooker Junction', as you must get a red before you are allowed a colour! Here, a New Street-bound Euston service with a Class 86 at the head has only got as far as Adderley Park. The footprints in the snow are a tell-tale sign that other trains have been stopped here with the driver de-training to get on the 'blower to the bobby'.

86225 *Hardwicke* arrives at Birmingham International on 14 April 1987 on a London Euston to Birmingham New Street working. (Andy Flowers Collection)

Left: **86258** *Talyllyn The First Preserved Railway* stands at Stafford on 17 March 1999 on a Manchester Piccadilly to Birmingham New Street CrossCountry service. (Andy Flowers Collection)

Below: **86229** *Lions Clubs International* passes Berkswell in July 2001 on a London Euston to Birmingham New Street service.

Rail Express Systems-liveried 86243 is seen passing Berkswell in July 2001 on a London Euston to Wolverhampton service.

Right: 86207 *City of Lichfield* awaits departure at Glasgow Central on 4 April 2000 on a Virgin CrossCountry service, the 12.30 to Poole. The Class 86/2 worked the train forward to Birmingham New Street with a Class 47/8 then taking over.

Below: 86244 *The Royal British Legion* stands at Manchester Piccadilly on 25 January 2000 on the 17.10 Virgin CrossCountry service to London Paddington.

Class 87s

The Class 87s were intended as a major advance in performance and, prior to the introduction of the new fleet, BR tested components of the locos on the Class 86s. Three 86/2s were upgraded with the planned frame-mounted GEC-412AZ traction motors and BP-9 bogies together with new electronic control equipment. Renumbered as 86101-03, these Class 86/1s delivered an increased output of 5,000hp and a higher maximum speed of 110mph, going on to be highly successful. When the new fleet was introduced, the trio could be used as substitutes for Class 87s but by 1995, they were non-standard and after time with CrossCountry, EWS and Freightliner, they were withdrawn from traffic. 86101 entered preservation, becoming the first preserved AC loco to work a timetabled service train after it was hired by Hull Trains for ECML work.

Above: 87016 *Willesden Intercity Depot* passes Berkswell in August 2002 on a Euston to Wolverhampton service hauling a rake of Virgin-liveried Mk.2s.

Left: On 11 September 2005, 87004 *Britannia* stands at Euston on a Birmingham New Street service for Virgin Trains.

After testing between Tring and Leighton Buzzard, the debut of the Class 87s was 1 June 1973 with a Longsight to Willesden Freightliner. Initial running showed the bogies needed to be adjusted to improve ride quality and the sanding gear was ineffective, with wheelslip higher than anticipated. After these teething issues, the class went on to become highly reliable and successful in service.

Before electrification to Glasgow was completed, the Class 87s showed their potential on services over the southern half of the West Coast. Upon completion of electrification, the new locos soon delivered excellent performance with trains of 12 coaches (around 430 tons) hauled up Shap and Beattock at a steady 90mph. Today's 'Voyagers' and 'Pendolinos' can maintain 100mph up both obstacles but at the time, the 90mph climbs with the '87s' were very impressive indeed.

87101 was built as a demonstration test bed for future technology, including thyristor control, but otherwise mirrored the layout of a standard Class 87, enabling use in normal traffic. It could be driven in 'ordinary' driving mode like the rest of the fleet or in 'advanced' using the new control technology. BR was initially dubious about interference to signalling from thyristor control, though in practice this was not an issue.

The move towards 110mph running in the 1980s meant further modifications to the Class 87s, including new Brecknell-Willis single arm pantographs, which were fitted between early 1984 and the end of 1988. From 1989 onwards, the class was fitted with Time Division Multiplex (TDM) push-pull equipment at Derby for working with the new DVTs replacing the ageing Mk.1 brake vans. Fitting of TDM equipment saw the distinctive multiple working cables removed from the cab fronts. Upon sectorisation, the Class 87/0s went to InterCity and 87101 went to Railfreight, although it still appeared occasionally on passenger trains. Virgin took control of the former InterCity fleet upon privatisation, although it soon unveiled plans to replace them with new tilting Class 390 'Pendolino' EMUs.

By the end of 2004, the remaining loco-hauled Euston–Northampton peak-time 'Cobbler' commuter services were being hauled by Class 90s, Virgin preferring to use Class 87s on its remaining long-distance loco-hauled services. As with most new trains, introduction of the 'Pendolinos' was delayed because of a number of modifications, the last one not being released from Washwood Heath until 2005. Virgin's final loco-hauled trains were due to be Class 87-hauled with Mk.3s and largely restricted to the Euston–Birmingham–Wolverhampton services. 87001 in BR Blue and Porterbrook-liveried 87002 were chosen as the final locos to be retained in service.

However, owing to low 'Pendolino' availability, Virgin needed to bring a loco-hauled diagram back in 2006, again with Class 87s. The final daytime Class 87 timetabled service on the WCML, excluding sleeper traffic, occurred on 22 December that year when 87002 hauled the 16.51 Euston to Birmingham and 19.00 return. Virgin commemorated the occasion by providing an 'Electric Scots 1973-2006' headboard. The driver also joined in, wearing an authentic 1970s BR uniform.

87002 stands at London Euston on 22 December 2006 after hauling the 16.51 Euston to Birmingham and 19.00 return, the last scheduled passenger services booked to be hauled by a Class 87 with Virgin Trains. A special 'Electric Scot 1973-2006' headboard was carried, with the driver getting in on the special occasion by wearing a 1970s British Rail uniform. The Class 87 is awaiting the road to take the empty stock to Wembley depot.

On 15 October 2008, 87002 *Royal Sovereign* stands at Birmingham International on the 'Electric Scot' railtour to Glasgow Central, the Class 87 by now essentially being a preserved loco. Failure of the battery charger on the return leg unfortunately saw assisting loco 57601 work the train back from Glasgow.

87001 *Stephenson* departs Milton Keynes on a Wolverhampton–London Euston service in August 2004.

87029 *Earl Marischal* stands at Stafford with a Preston to London Euston service in February 2000.

87020 *North Briton* stands at Wolverhampton with a service for London Euston in February 2000.

87015 *Howard of Effingham* stands at Crewe in June 1990 on a Liverpool to Euston service. The loco has been run-round the train and is hauling the DVT forwards because of TDM issues, a common problem in the early years of using Driving Van Trailers.

87006 passes Canley on 16 June 2006, working the 16.52 London Euston to Birmingham New Street. The loco had previously spent a short time on trial with DRS as it trialled electrically hauled intermodal services and was still carrying the company's dark blue base colour. When taken back on lease by Virgin, this was augmented with full yellow cabs, as seen here.

87014 *Knight of the Thistle* prepares to propel the 17.50 Preston–Euston south from Crewe on 31 December 1999.

87015 *Howard of Effingham* departs Rugby with a Birmingham New Street–London Euston service in June 2000, the stock being the normal Mk.2 coaches employed on the West Midlands services.

87020 *North Briton* pauses at Edinburgh Haymarket on 15 February 2000, on the 10.31 Birmingham International to Edinburgh Waverley service. Class 87s were relatively uncommon at Edinburgh, other than for a few years when they were booked on the Caledonian Sleeper services, though they made occasional appearances on CrossCountry services such as here.

Ex-works 87019 *Sir Winston Churchill* departs Rugby in July 2000 on a London Euston to Manchester Piccadilly service.

87003 *Patriot* leaves Crewe on a London Euston to Manchester Piccadilly service in June 2001.

InterCity 250

BR was not ready for the 1980s recession and an increase in domestic air travel. Passenger numbers went down and without speed improvements through the APT, the decision was made to upgrade services to 110mph running. The 'Royal Scot', originally a five-hour timing after electrification through to Glasgow, had slowed to five hours and 15 minutes. The Mk.3s and Class 87s were capable of 110mph running, but to enable this in the absence of new stock, some Mk.1 Full Brakes were upgraded for higher speed from 1984. Stock to replace the Mk.1s came in the form of Mk.3b DVTs, ordered in January 1986.

Following a series of tests, it was surmised that the Class 89 prototype was not suitable as a high-speed locomotive, being unable to run at speeds of 125mph as planned for much of the route south of Crewe and a tilt solution was needed. With little advantage over existing Class 87s, no follow-on orders for the Class 89 were forthcoming, although a new high-speed electric loco was still wanted by BR to speed up WCML services.

A mixed traffic loco was specified, 25 in total, which would be capable of powering 750 tonne freights over Shap and Beattock and of haulage tilting and conventional passenger stock when required. The wide remit of the loco was later downgraded as technological limitations became apparent, though delivery was still planned for 1991. GEC was awarded the contract for 31 Class 91s for the ECML in February 1986 with an option for 25 more for the WCML. A submission for tilting Mk.4 coaches was discussed by BR in the mid-1980s but was rejected. Without tilting coaches, the new locos would show no advantage over Class 90s running at 110mph, so the WCML option was never taken up for the Class 91s.

After the withdrawal of the APTs, the fastest trains on the WCML were three HST sets for Euston–Holyhead traffic. Comparisons with the East Coast became even more pronounced following completion of electrification between Edinburgh and King's Cross in 1991. To even out the speed and travel quality, BR developed the InterCity 250 project to replace conventional loco-hauled passenger services on the WCML. This envisaged a high-speed Class 93 electric locomotive with

APT 370002 arrives into Preston in August 1981 while working a scheduled London Euston to Glasgow timetabled working, the waiting passengers showing a close interest in their brand-new train. Low passenger loadings and high maintenance costs saw the sets last only a few short years in sporadic service.

push-pull Mk.5 stock and a DVT, a design that was essentially an upgrade of the Class 91 and Mk.4 sets in service on the ECML. Trains would be limited to 125mph, with the prospect of 155mph running with in-cab signalling.

The Class 93 project progressed as far as BR issuing a tender for locos and stock in March 1991 with delivery planned for 1995. Favoured bidders were likely to be ABB Traction, GEC-Alsthom or Siemens. With track and technological issues together with a lack of financial backing from the government, the project was cancelled in July 1992, although some of the planning was used to set requirements for the WCML upgrade carried out under Railtrack and Network Rail.

Class 90s

With BR striving to remain competitive, it became clear that new locomotives would be needed to run more services at 110mph. The government authorised funding for 29 new locos in 1985, with the award for construction given to BREL at Crewe. In 1987, as differences from Class 87s became clear, the designation was changed to Class 90 and the order increased to 50 locos.

On 22 December 2004, EWS Class 90 90026, on hire to Virgin West Coast, awaits departure at Euston on a Wolverhampton service.

90028 departs from Milton Keynes in August 2005 on a Wolverhampton to London Euston service. Virgin regularly hired in EWS Class 90s to supplement its own fleet of 15 locos prior to the introduction of the 'Pendolinos'.

In 2014, Direct Rail Services unveiled a Class 90 in its dark blue livery, with the loco hired to Virgin Trains for two years for use on its 'Pretendolino' Mk.3 set. In October 2014, 90034 stands at Coventry on the 20.50 Birmingham New Street to London Euston service.

Carrying an experimental and one-off Railfreight Distribution livery and now with additional EWS brandings, 90036 departs from Coventry in August 2007 with a New Street–Euston service. The loco had been hired in by Virgin Trains.

90008 *The Birmingham Royal Ballet* flies through the centre road at Rugby on 21 March 2002, on the 13.00 London Euston to Liverpool Lime Street.

90045, resplendent in the revised green and yellow Freightliner livery, stands at London Euston on the 'Pretendolino' set and ready to work to Preston on the 1P05 18.46 departure on 30 December 2010.

90047, in original two-tone Railfreight grey with Freightliner branding, stands at London Euston on the 'Pretendolino' set with the 14.43 departure to Birmingham New Street on 18 January 2011.

90003 stands at Carlisle on the southern end of a late West Coast service on 25 May 1993. The loco had been run-round owing to problems with the DVT, 82117 in this instance. (Andy Flowers Collection)

Freightliner Class 90/1 90146 stands at Crewe on 30 March 2000 on the 17.10 Glasgow Central to London Euston.

90015 *The International Brigades* stands at the bufferstops at Euston in February 2000, after arriving on a service from Birmingham New Street. The Class 90 was dragging the DVT owing to TDM issues.

EWS-liveried 90020 approaches Canley on a London Euston to Birmingham New Street service on 27 May 2009, the stock and loco substituting for an unavailable 'Pendolino' unit.

GNER-liveried 90024 stands at Nuneaton on 19 June 2003. The '90' had been repainted into the East Coast Main Line operator's livery with a view to its use on hire, although, in the event, the loco spent almost as much time on the WCML as the east and also appeared on the Great Eastern Main Line on Norwich–Liverpool Street services. Class 86 86229 *Lions Clubs International* waits at the rear.

Building of the Class 91s for the ECML delayed completion of the Class 90 fleet, and it was September 1988 before 90001 was sent to Derby for initial testing. The first appearance in service was 90005 in March 1988 on a VIP special from Euston to Northampton. The first working of a Class 90 on a timetabled service train was 90003 on 12 July 1988, it taking the 13.46 Blackpool to Euston forward from Preston. Sectorisation by BR saw the mixed traffic fleet of Class 90s split between freight and passenger operators with 15 going to InterCity, five to Parcels (soon to become Rail Express Systems) and 30 to Railfreight Distribution. RfD's allocation was later split between EWS and Freightliner and the same 15 passenger Class 90s remained in similar use until 2020, having transferred to East Anglia following the end of their use with Virgin.

Third generation electrics

In 1986, Crewe built the Brush-designed Class 89 Co-Co, which featured on some test trains on the WCML, being allocated to Crewe in 1987. Testing was mostly between Crewe and Carlisle, although some runs were further south. The loco was also tested over Beattock on the BREL International coaches with the 'Prometheus' test car. A proposed freight version of the '89', dubbed Class 88 at the time, was never built.

Class 91s, while dedicated to the East Coast Main Line, have appeared on the West Coast on a few occasions with regular turns over some stretches. On 30 April 1992, 91012 carried out a press run from Euston to Birmingham Heartlands, which was a proposed site for a new interchange station to serve Birmingham and situated on the line from Stechford to Aston. The train recorded a very quick time from Euston to Birmingham of 71 minutes and nine seconds, with Coventry passed in 57 minutes. Another run to Birmingham took place on 29 June 1993 with 91001 and set BN74.

The '91s' were also used on special test workings between Glasgow and Carlisle in 1989. InterCity West Coast was widely reported to have proposed to use £150m, made available through government funding released in 1993, to lease 15 Class 91s and Mk.4 rakes for key WCML services, although the project was abandoned. Further demonstration runs were made from London Euston with Class and Mk.4s to Birmingham, Manchester, Carlisle and Liverpool in June 1993. These 'IC225 Awareness Specials' included Carlisle on 28 June 1993.

On 2 March 1997, 91027 was on the West Coast on a Virgin CrossCountry service, formed of a rake of East Coast Mk4s, this replacing two Class 158 Sprinters on an Edinburgh to Manchester Airport service and which terminated at Carlisle. Class 91s were due to become common on the WCML from May 2021, after open access operator Grand Union announced plans for the introduction of a Stirling to Euston service via Motherwell and the WCML. These plans were later postponed indefinitely because of COVID-19.

The Class 92s, were built between 1992 and 1996 by Brush as a dual mode (third rail and overhead AC) loco with the capability of travelling over the whole of the UK's electrified network, including the Channel Tunnel. On the WCML, Class 92s took years to gain authorisation to operate because of issues with signalling interference from the electronically complex machines.

The introduction of new Mk.5 stock for the Caledonian Sleeper operation saw GBRf-owned Class 92s specified as the motive power. Poor availability initially saw Class 90s used to bolster the fleet on the existing Mk.3 stock but the introduction of a full fleet of Mk.5s in 2019 saw Class 92s take full control following reliability modifications.

On 25 March 2020, 88006 *Juno* **passes Cathiron, just north of Rugby, working the 4M26 05.46 Mossend to Daventry intermodal service for DRS. Despite long-standing rumours that the Class 88 fleet may take over from Class 92s on the Caledonian Sleeper services, the modern bi-mode electric locos are yet to have any booked passenger duties, instead working container and nuclear fuel traffic for DRS.**

Class 91s were an everyday sight in Glasgow until relatively recently on through services from the East Coast Main Line via Edinburgh and Carstairs. 91025 arrives at Glasgow Central on the 11.00 GNER service from London King's Cross on 4 April 2000.

DRS' ten dual-mode Class 88s were introduced primarily for freight on the WCML with an eye to the charter passenger market. At the time of writing, none of the fleet has worked a timetabled passenger service but they are in demand for railtours and heritage railway diesel galas. The type's first revenue earning service following test runs was Belmond's Northern Belle on 9 May 2017 with 88002 powering the 1Z88 09.32 VIP launch special from Euston to Carlisle.

With the Class 93 numbers not used following the abandonment of the InterCity 250 project, the recent £40m order of ten tri-mode locomotives to be built by Stadler Rail in Valencia will be numbered 93001-93010. The overhead electric, battery, and diesel locomotives, ordered by the Rail Operations Group (ROG) and leased from Beacon Rail, will feature a top speed of 110mph with an output of 5,438hp on electric power and 1,800hp on hybrid (diesel/battery). They feature the larger Caterpillar C32 V12 power unit, compared to the C27 V12 in the Class 88s. Before COVID-19, they were due for delivery from August 2020 although this is now put back to early 2023. The Class 93s are planned for use on passenger charter and freight work together with a possible new Rail Express operation.

In the years before Class 92s became regular performers on the Caledonian Sleepers, they had no booked passenger duties and were in great demand on enthusiasts railtours. On 20 July 2002, 92002 *H.G. Wells* with 56069 in tow stands at Carlisle on the 'Ayr Receder' tour. The Class 92 worked the multi-traction excursion forward to Mossend Yard, where the Class 56 took over.

Though now largely restricted to sleeper duties when seen on the West Coast Main Line, Class 92s were regular performers on freight duties in the late 1990s and 2000s after issues with electrical interference with signalling had been resolved. 92005 *Mozart* passes Cathiron in June 2002 on a Mossend to Daventry service. This traffic was largely taken over by Class 90s when EWS was taken over by DB Schenker.

Chapter 7
Records & Performance

The hilly northern stretches of the WCML required locos with high power outputs to keep time, and the battle for speed on Anglo-Scottish services with operators on the more favourably graded and aligned ECML saw ever more powerful designs introduced. Dugal Drummond's 4-4-0s of 1884 were widely regarded as some of the most advanced steam locomotives in the world. The Caledonian set power output records when Drummond built two 4-4-0s in 1889 with the boiler pressure increased from 150lb per square inch to 200lb. giving an output figure of 940hp at 51mph. The follow-on 'Dunalastair' 4-4-0 Class also gave strong performances.

One of the LNWR's 'Claughton' 4-6-0s on test in 1913 gave an output of 1,669hp approaching Tebay at 69mph, which was a record up until the time of larger locos following the grouping of 1923. Following the success of the Stanier 'Pacifics' in 1938, the LMS planned a more ambitious development, a streamlined, four-cylinder 4-6-4 with a 300lb pressure boiler and a 70ft^2 mechanically fired grate. Concerns regarding gauging and costs, together with plans for modern traction, meant the ambitious design never appeared.

Performance compared

Before Birmingham International opened, inter-regional services for Paddington or the south coast were routed via Solihull. Since 1976, cross-country traffic, together with Euston services over the WCML between Coventry and Birmingham, have seen a wide variety of motive power. Passed for 100mph running and with a fast exit from Coventry, the line offers a great opportunity to compare traction performance, which is what the author did, in 2001. As well as fulfilling the criteria in terms of variety, the section is also graded to allow high speeds, straight and rising at 1 in 330 up to Beechwood Tunnel then falling at the same grade over the second half of the run, giving traction the opportunity to show its paces.

The findings are summarised in the following graphs and are the best runs timed with each loco. Some runs were one-offs, such as the Class 59. Comparison of performance between different types of traction is always difficult. Although most trains were seven air-conditioned Mk.2 coaches, some were just six (the Class 33, 47, 50 and Type 5s) and the Class 20s had a dead Class 47 in tow. Nevertheless, the results are worthy of analysis.

There were few major surprises; locos with higher horsepower were better in terms of speed, acceleration and overall running time, although a few exceptions were noted. D9000, showed the relative sluggishness of the class away from a standing start, with the second power unit not kicking in until well underway to reduce the risk of overloading. Surprisingly, a pair of Class 31/4s showed they could accelerate quickly and sustain speeds in the mid-90s.

From the graphs, the Class 59 was the best freight Type 5 performer, although it was driven hard, the pair of Class 31s were almost as quick as a single '47' and the single Class 31 was only just shaded by the Class 33 in acceleration and running time. Everything up to Classes 47 and 50 was driven flat out but AC electrics and D9000 were eased off once they reached 100mph. Class 87s in particular have been noted along the line at speeds of over 110mph.

Acceleration (Passing Time to Canley)

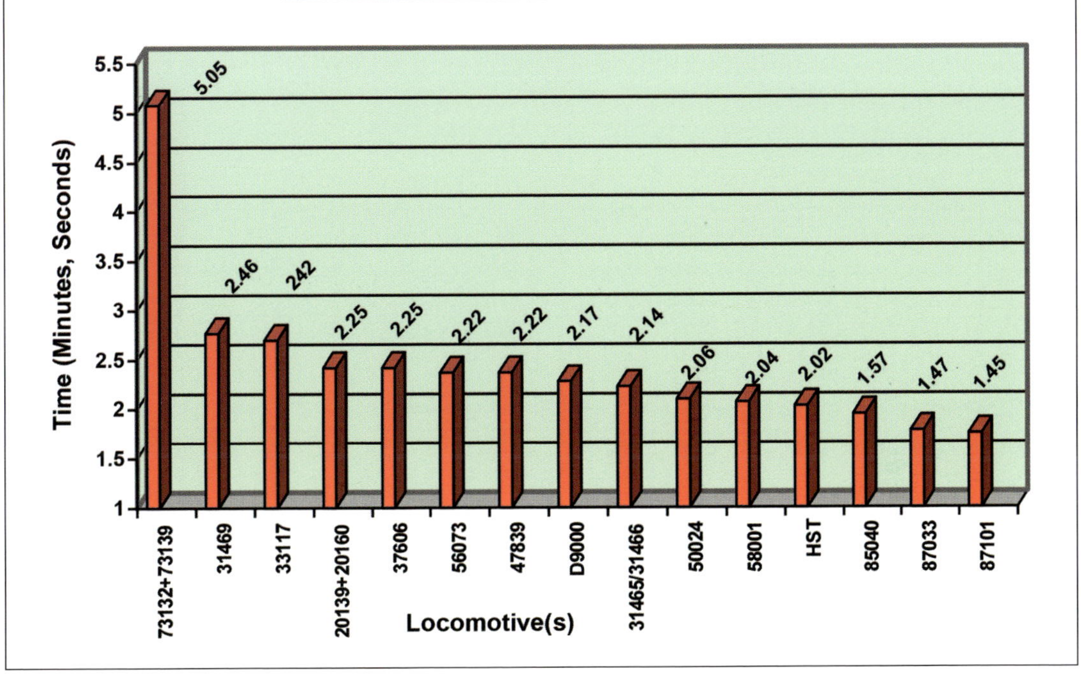

Locomotive(s)	Time (Minutes, Seconds)
73132+73139	5.05
31469	2.46
33117	2.42
20139+20160	2.25
37606	2.25
56073	2.22
47839	2.22
D9000	2.17
31465/31466	2.14
50024	2.06
58001	2.04
HST	2.02
85040	1.57
87033	1.47
87101	1.45

Overall Running Time (Coventry to Birmingham International)

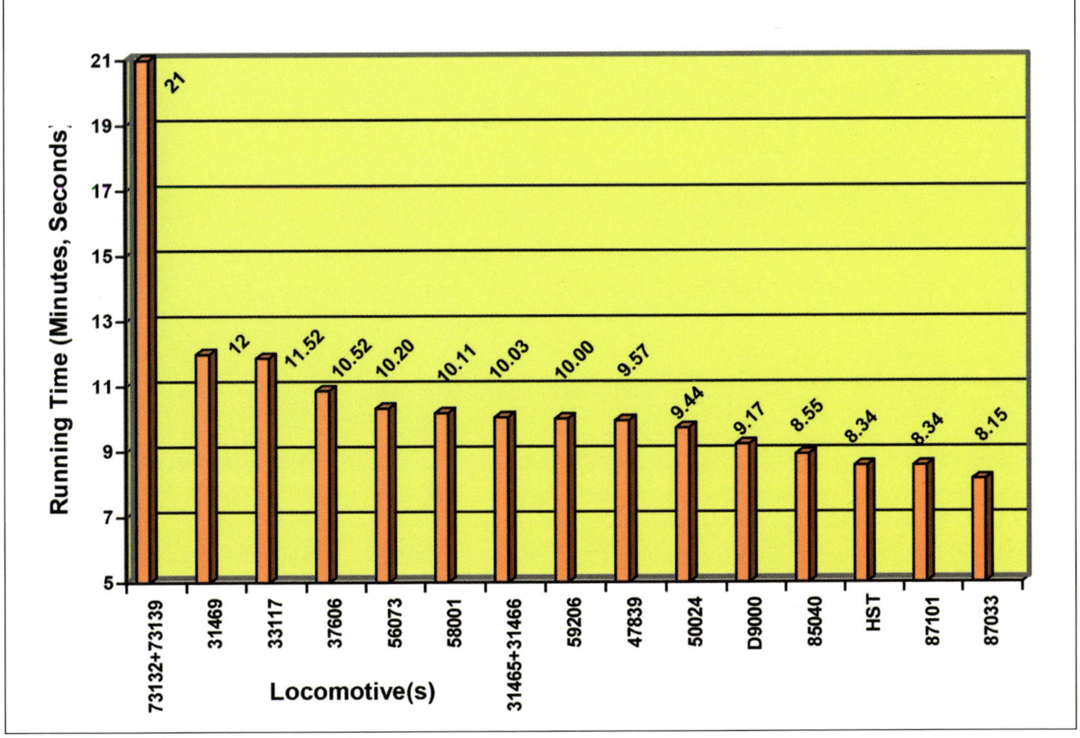

Locomotive(s)	Running Time (Minutes, Seconds)
73132+73139	21
31469	12
33117	11.52
37606	10.52
56073	10.20
58001	10.11
31465+31466	10.03
59206	10.00
47839	9.57
50024	9.44
D9000	9.17
85040	8.55
HST	8.34
87101	8.34
87033	8.15

West Coast Main Line Locomotive Haulage

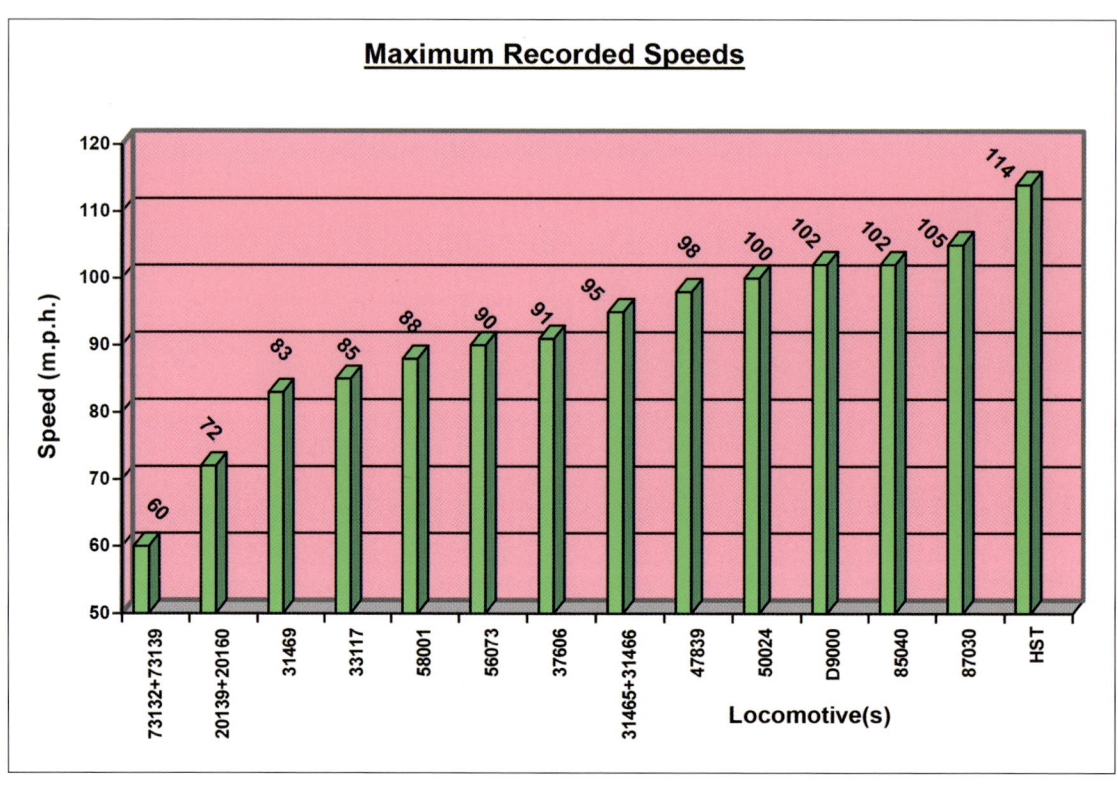

Chapter 8
New Operators

The return of daytime loco-hauled services over the WCML with open access operator Grand Central was expected in 2020. These would have run between Blackpool and Euston using Class 90s and four rakes of six Mk.4 coaches, operating at speeds of up to 110mph. Grand Central initially applied to the Office of Rail Regulation (ORR) to run these services in November 2010 using Class 67s and Mk.3 coaches. However, the ORR rejected this bid on the basis that it would not attract new revenue, just take passengers away from the franchise operator Virgin Trains.

A revised bid to the ORR was lodged in October 2017, this being approved in June 2018 with a seven-year track access agreement. The new service was set to feature five trains each way Mondays to Saturdays, calling at stops between Blackpool and Preston, then Nuneaton and Milton Keynes. A service of four trains in each direction would also operate on Sundays while there was an option for a sixth daily service included in the track access agreement.

The £21m investment included the lease of 24 Mk.4s from Eversholt Rail until December 2026 and a £1.5m refurbishment of the stock, which was carried out by Alstom in Widnes. The coaches would also be maintained by Alstom at Wembley depot. Grand Central hired five Class 90s from DB Cargo, to be maintained at Crewe Electric, with three to be diagrammed each day, one on maintenance and one on standby with the spare set. The first '90' to be repainted in the new Grand Central livery was 90026 at Toton, which was revealed to the press at Crewe in February 2020. The full GC Class 90 fleet was due to comprise 90021, 90026, 90029, 90039 and 90040. Initially, Class 91s were planned for the new services but were unavailable as they were expected to still be in use on the East Coast Main Line at the start date because of delays in delivering the Hitachi Class 800s.

Two DB Class 90s not in the dedicated fleet, 90019 and 90036, carried out a test and training run to Blackpool with a rake of Mk.4s on 4 March 2020, these operating in top and tail mode at that stage (the DVT being temporarily out of action on the day). 90036 led into Blackpool, becoming the first Class 90 to reach the Lancashire seaside town under its own power; one '90' had got to Blackpool before, dead in train on a Euston service and hauled by a Class 47.

However, Grand Central had to suspend its East Coast train services from Friday 3 April 2020, owing to the impact of COVID-19 on public transport. Crew training on the new stock was also halted for the same reason with the service start initially postponed until May 2021. As the impact of the pandemic became clearer, Arriva-owned Grand Central abandoned its plans for Blackpool services with the announcement coming in October 2020. The Grand Central Class 90s were returned to DB while the Mk.4 stock has now been leased to Transport for Wales and will eventually be used to expand its loco-hauled operation with Class 67s.

The future
Despite the open access failure, the future of locomotive haulage on the West Coast Main Line is secure for the next few years, on charter work at least, after Locomotive Services Limited bought 87002 and 86101 following the end of the contract for haulage of the Caledonian Sleepers as the overnight services turned fully to Mk.5 stock, which is capable of haulage by Class 73/9s and Class 92s only in normal traffic.

On Friday 26 June 2020, 90026 and 90029 are seen at Cathiron working top and tail on a Grand Central stock transfer from Widnes to Wembley, this conveying two sets of newly refurbished Mk.4 stock.

LSL is expanding its charter work under its Saphos and Statesman marketing brands and hopes to use a mix of Classes 86, 87 and 90 on West Coast charter passenger services, having also acquired 90001 and 90002 from Porterbrook. These have all been repainted into InterCity colours along with a matching set of Mk.3 coaches and DVTs displaced from East Anglia.

LSL also owns and operates a wide-ranging diesel fleet including Class 08s, 37s, 47s, the Blue Pullman HST set and a Deltic (D9000), all based at its Crewe depot for easy access onto the main line. D9016 is also owned but stored out of use in Margate. Additionally, in 2018, Class 40 D213 (40013) joined the fleet on a three-year lease, which is likely to be extended following COVID-19.

Despite the cancelled reintroduction of daylight locomotive-hauled services, the next few years should see opportunities for enthusiasts to travel behind and photograph locomotives on 'The Premier Line'. With an ever-changing railway, introduction of new loco-hauled services cannot be ruled out and we look forward to further developments.